ENDORSEMENTS

Dr. James Davis and Dr. Timothy Hill have brought together their years of experience into this exciting and challenging book. The phrase "finish well" is often heard, but seldom is there practical advice on how one goes about running and finishing the race of life. This book does that with a solid biblical foundation and insights from two men who are effectively running "the heavenly race!"

—**Dr. Doug Beacham**, General Superintendent,
International Pentecostal Holiness Church

Each one of us is part of a significant journey, but the heavenly race is the one that truly counts. This is the message of this new book by two of the most enlightened, visionary, mission-minded and forward-thinking leaders of this generation. Drs. Timothy Hill and James O. Davis synergize their dynamism, wisdom, and experience to bring forth a work of this magnitude. It promises to leave a lasting impression on every future-looking leader who aspires to be a finisher and have a lasting impact and a role in completing the Great Commission. As someone who was deeply impacted by these two great global church statesman, I enthusiastically recommend *The Heavenly Race: The Future Belongs to the Finisher*, to all my friends and church leaders.

—**Rev. Florin Cimpean**, Administrative Bishop,
Church of God Romanian Territory, Senior Pastor,
Philadelphia Romanian Church of God

Our belief in God's commitment to complete His Great Commission also means that God is right now calling people of all ages, stages, vocations, and even locations to be pastors, evangelists, preachers, and missionaries, to take the Good News of Jesus Christ to every person in the world. This is why Christian leaders must be committed to calling out the called repeatedly. This book will ignite you to do it!

—**Ronnie W. Floyd**, Pastor, Author, Ministry Strategist, and Pastor Emeritus of Cross Church

I highly recommend this book written by Dr. Tim Hill and Dr. James Davis. These men are highly regarded as men of the gospel who have a burden and desire to finish the Great Commission. All young ministers need this book in their hands to catch the vision to evangelize the world.

—**Keith Ivester**, National Overseer of Canada (COG)

Jesus said, "The harvest truly is plentiful, but the laborers are few. Therefore pray the Lord of the harvest to send out laborers into His harvest." If there are two men who have it on their hearts to see laborers raised up to help finish the Great Commission, it is Dr. James O. Davis and Dr. Timothy Hill. *The Heavenly Race: The Future Belongs to the Finisher*, is a textbook, a handbook that will inspire, encourage, and equip the raising up of those much-needed laborers Jesus encouraged us to pray about. I recommend this book to all who have a burden for this lost world to turn back to Christ in order to see the words of Christ fulfilled—"the gospel shall be preached to all nations, then the end shall come."

—**Rev. Peter Mortlock**, Founder, City Impact Churches, Auckland, New Zealand

Turn your dreams into reality with a road map to success. In *The Heavenly Race: The Future Belongs to the Finisher*, Drs. Hill and Davis give you the tools to transform your aspirations into achievements. Their actionable GOALS framework breaks down the goal-setting process, empowering you to strategize effectively, execute efficiently, and fulfill your purpose. Whether it's a personal quest or a ministry mission, this wise and handy guide by two celebrated "pros" equips you to navigate the path from big dream to blacktopped destination.

—**Dr. Leonard Sweet**, Prolific Author, Preacher, Professor, Publisher (salishsea.press) and Proprietor

Every person in ministry should read this book! I wish I could have read it 40 years ago! I promise, if you follow the teaching of these two spiritual giants in this book, you will finish well!

—**Dr. Benny Tate**, Senior Pastor, Rock Springs Church, Milner, Georgia

Our church family's leadership is passionately committed to sacrificially serving a younger generation of called ones. We share a clarity that God has called each young woman and man to know Him and to be equipped with ministry gifts to serve the church and the mission it is commissioned to do. My colleagues Dr. Timothy Hill and Dr. James O. Davis in *The Heavenly Race: The Future Belongs to the Finisher* draw on their wealth of experience and wisdom to provide exactly that—equipping and encouraging for a current generation of younger leaders to confidently live their lives and calling for their Lord. My advice: Engage the wisdom, live the truths shared.

—**Rev. David Wells, M.A., D.D.**, President-Pentecostal Charismatic Churches of North America (PCCNA), General Superintendent – The Pentecostal Assemblies of Canada (PAOC), David.Wells@paoc.org

THE
HEAVENLY
RACE

The FUTURE BELONGS to the FINISHER

TIMOTHY HILL & JAMES O. DAVIS

Foreword by JENTEZEN FRANKLIN

DEDICATION

Reverend John W. Hill, the father of Dr. Timothy Hill,
who mentored young preachers, multiplied his disciples,
and ministered to all peoples.
His legacy is forever established.

Dr. Robert E. Coleman, Mentor of Dr. James O. Davis,
who authored the best-selling book, *The Master Plan of
Evangelism*, served as distinguishing professor at Trinioy
Evangelical Divinity School, Gordon-Conway,
and Asbury Seminary.

CONTENTS

Foreword xv

Introduction xvii

  A. Gather the Facts xviii

  B. Organize a Plan xix

  C. Act on the Plan xxi

  D. Look Back and Review xxii

  E. Set New Goals xxiii

Chapter 1: The Contest Before Us 1

  A. Exchange Unworthy Goals with Worthy Goals 6

  B. Exchange Unclear Goals with Clear Goals 6

  C. Exchange Unbalanced Goals with Balanced
    Goals 7

    1. There Is a Difference 8

    2. There Is a Discipline 8

    3. There Is a Dividend 8

    4. There Is a Direction 8

    5. There Is a Disqualification 8

Chapter 2: The Crowds Around Us 9

  A. Worshiping Faith: Abel 10

  B. Witnessing Faith: Enoch 10

  C. Working Faith: Noah 11

  D. Walking Faith: Abraham 12

  E. Waiting Faith: Sarah 13

F. Willing Faith: Isaac.. 14

G. Wrestling Faith: Jacob.. 14

H. Wishing Faith: Joseph... 15

I. Wisdom Faith: Moses' Parents 16

J. Weighing Faith: Moses 17

K. Warring Faith: Joshua.. 18

L. Welcoming Faith: Rahab 19

M. Winning Faith: Gideon, Barak, Samson, Jephthah, David, Samuel, Prophets 20

N. Wandering Faith: Persecuted and Martyred 21

Chapter 3: The Conditioning Within Us 23

A. Things That Slow Us Down.................................... 23

B. Things That Trip Us Up.. 26

Chapter 4: The Course Before Us... 31

A. The Characteristics of a Ministry Calling............... 33

1. Providential.. 33

2. Purposeful 33

3. Personal 34

4. Practical 35

5. Powerful 36

6. Perplexing 36

B. The Confirmation of a Ministry Calling................. 37

C. The Continuation of a Ministry Calling................. 38

Chapter 5: The Continuation Before Us 41

A. We Need Fuel for the Journey 42

1. Know Your Limits 42

2. Read the Gauges.. 43

3. Keep Up with your Own Maintenance............ 43

4. Correcting Your Course.................................... 44

B. We Need to Keep On Keeping On in the Journey.. 45

C. The Journey Will Usually Take Longer Than We Think 46

D. Here's Some Fuel for You.................................... 47

1. Trust Your Trainer 48

2. Pace Instead of Race 48

3. Be Consistent and Steady............................ 49

4. Build Your Courage................................... 49

5. Listen for the Cheers of Your Fans.................. 49

6. Remember You Can't Lose 49

Chapter 6: The Coach to Us.................................51

A. Our Master and Mentor 51

B. Our Measurement and Motivation....................... 54

1. Renewal 54

2. Rejoice 54

3. Rest... 55

4. Reflect 55

C. The Principle of Concentration 56

D. The Principle of Cancellation 57

E. The Principle of Continuation 57

Chapter 7: The Crown for Us 61

A. The Imperishable Crown
(1 Corinthians 9:24-25) 63

B. The Crown of Rejoicing (1 Thessalonians 2:19)..... 63

C. The Crown of Righteousness (2 Timothy 4:8)........ 64

D. The Crown of Glory (1 Peter 5:40) 65

E. The Crown of Life (Revelation 2:10)............... 65

F. Picture This Image................................ 68

1. Read Your Map Before You Leave Home 69

2. Stop at Red Lights 69

3. Yield the Right-of-way to Others............ 69

4. Go at Green Lights......................... 69

Conclusion..71

A. Finding Christ in the Heavenly Race............... 72

1. Apprehend 72

2. Apprehensive................................ 73

B. Following Christ in the Heavenly Race 73

1. Concentration on the Present................. 73

2. Obliteration of the Past.................... 75

3. Pressing Toward the Mark 76

    C. Finishing for Christ in the Heavenly Race..............77
        1. The Mark to Reach................................77
        2. The Medal to Reward...........................77

**Appendix 1: How Can I Know God Called
Me to Preach? 83**
    A. Compulsion...84
    B. Counsel 85
    C. Concern...86
    D. Communication......................................87
    E. Constraint...88
    F. Contrition...88
    G. Confirmation...89

**Appendix 2: Living and Leading Worthy
of Your Calling 93**
    A. How the Gifts Are Delivered....................94
    B. How the Gifts Are Described 96
        1. Wisdom (1 Corinthians 12:8) 97
        2. Knowledge (1 Corinthians 12:8).........97
        3. Faith by the same Spirit
           (1 Corinthians 12:9)............................97
        4. Healing by the one Spirit
           (1 Corinthians 12:9)............................97
        5. Miracles (1 Corinthians 12:10) 97
        6. Prophecy (1 Corinthians 12:10)..........97
        7. Distinguishing of Spirits 98
        8. Various Kinds of Tongues/Interpretation of
           Tongues (1 Corinthians 12:10) 98
        9. Teachers (1 Corinthians 12:28)...........98
       10. Exhortation (Romans 12:6,8) 98
       11, Giving (Romans 12:6,8). 98
       12. Leading (Romans 12:6,8). 98
       13. Mercy (Romans 12:6,8) 98
    C. How the Gifts Are Developed 99
    D. How the Gifts Are Displayed 101
        1. Stature (Ephesians 4:13)....................102

   2. Stability (Ephesians 4:14)................................. 102

   3. Speech (Ephesians 4:15).................................... 102

   4. Service (Ephesians 4:16).................................... 103

About the Authors... **105**

FOREWORD

The late renowned author Mark Twain said, "The two most important days in your life are the day you are born and the day you find out why." People from all walks of life and in every world region at some point look inwardly and ask, "Is there more to my life than this? Can I truly make a significant difference?"

Once we have come to Christ, repenting of our sins, He places us in a heavenly race. We are not in the heavenly race in order to be saved; it was salvation that qualified us to be in the race. We are not running in this race so we can go to heaven. Our Lord has drafted us into this race to fulfill why we were born before our life comes to a close.

In *The Heavenly Race: The Future Belongs to the Finisher*, you will learn firsthand how to *find, follow,* and *finish* the will of God. Dr. Timothy Hill, General Overseer of the Church of God, and Dr. James O. Davis, Founder/President of the Global Church Network, have synergized their wisdom and writing to bring to you a masterful, thought-through ministry leadership book that will save you countless years, wasted money, and lost time.

When it comes to finding, you will come to know your God-given, divine call for impacting this generation. You will move from being a wondering generality to a definite specific. Your course will be clear, and your ministry career will be successful.

When it comes to following, you will learn the quintessential commitments required to getting into this heavenly race and staying in it until you are standing in the Christian's winning circle. You will find that *The Heavenly Race* will be a training guide that you will refer to time and time again, throughout the seasons of your life.

After you have understood the finding and undertook the following, you will be prepared to break the tape, finishing successfully. The future belongs to the finisher! When we begin with the finish in mind, our focus is on the future and what and how it will take to achieve the goals the Lord has placed in our hearts.

Finding is about our calling. Following is about commitment and continuation. Finishing is about our completion. Finishing is not about dying and taking our rightful place in the grandstand of Glory. It is about finishing God's will and then joining the heavenly hosts of saints of past, present, and future. This is what *The Heavenly Race* brings into precise perspective for us. Your ministry will be deeper, your thoughts clearer, and your faith stronger.

Dr. Hill and Dr. Davis have crisscrossed this world, traveling millions of miles, preaching the gospel, equipping both young and seasoned ministers with the focus on finishing the Great Commission. I am honored to pen this foreword and to recommend *The Heavenly Race: The Future Belongs to the Finisher* to you. You are challenged to find, follow, and finish God's will for your life! You hold in your hand a powerful compass, showing you the right direction for a powerful, transforming ministry for decades to come.

—Rev. Jentezen Franklin
Senior Pastor, Free Chapel,
Gainesville, Georgia
April 2024

INTRODUCTION

The future always belongs to the finisher. This principle is true and accurate, whether it be a small task on our list or a huge project that we are undertaking in life. The future belongs to the finisher.

Think about it with me for a moment. Is it not true that your personal philosophy, whatever it may be right now, has accurately provided for you what it was intended to provide for you? We are not called to live a fatalistic life, whatever will come our way, will come our way. We're called to make projections about the future, create a path in the present, and take the needed steps forward to success. Every great adventure begins with that first step. And that first step is sometimes the most important one.

Everything in life has a beginning point and an ending point; and one of the greatest life lessons to learn, especially early in life, is to begin with the end in mind. When we're younger we're just trying to take the next step without thinking about what the curvature of the Earth is bringing to us with each new day. We spend more time climbing and clocking than we do compassing. What would it be like if you could begin with the end in mind? What would it be like if you could get married with the end in mind? What would it be like if you could begin a ministry with the end in mind?

We learned a long time ago that if we can develop a simple process for projects of personal well-being, then we will be far more multipliable in our lives. Often we want to make the simple complex instead of simplifying the complicated. What made Einstein so famous? It was not that he had a brilliant mind, but that he was able to make the complex simple. Who hasn't heard of $E=mc^2$?

A vision becomes a goal when we put a date on it.

A vision becomes a goal when we put a date on it. Until we set a date, it's only blue-sky talk, not a practical walk. Many people like to talk about vision, but they never achieve very much with the vision. If we're ever going to achieve something that's grand, then it will begin with a goal.

Every goal doesn't have to be a God-sized goal. God has a God-sized goal for the world. For God so loved the world. If we cast our vision to the stars, we will land on the moon. If we cast our vision on the trees, we will hit the ground. There is an overarching art to casting vision. Yet, in this vision are measurable goals.

If you're going to finish, we suggest that you're going to have to be able to develop measurable goals and execute them in a timely manner. With that in mind, **GOALS** is an acronym for us. Once you have learned this acronym and have been able to apply it numerous times, it will become like a wheel that you will roll in your decision-making, your planning, and your vision casting.

GATHER THE FACTS

For us to turn our vision into a measurable goal, we have to begin with research. We've been accused of a lot of things in life, no doubt, but one thing we've never been accused of is knowing too much. We often say, study yourself to death, and pray yourself back to life again! We have to do our research. We have to learn to ask the right questions to get the right answers. We have to learn to be in the right room with the right people to gain the right wisdom.

If you don't have a target, you're never going to hit it.

We have to research as it relates to the amount of *money* that we will need, the kind of *mindset* that we will need to develop, the kind of *members* that we will need to have in our life, and the kind of *motivation* required to stay in the race until we cross the finish line. We will attract who we are, not what we want.

ORGANIZE A PLAN

Someone has said: "If you fail to plan, then you're planning to fail." People will always be subject to someone else who has a plan. We're either fulfilling our plan and our goals or we are fulfilling someone else's plan and goals. Of course, as a Christ follower, we are living our lives to help fulfill the goals that God has for this earth, and that Christ has for us in life and ministry.

When we sit down and begin to think about our plan, we need to have certain targets. Many young leaders like to shoot the arrow and move the target according to where the arrow is going. Yet, this is a reactionary lifestyle, not a proactive leadership.

If you don't have a target, you're never going to hit it. Jack Nicholas, one of the greatest, if not the greatest legendary golfer of all time, was asked, "Are there some long putts that you think you're not going to make?"

He said, "If I didn't think I was going to make it, the odds are, I never will. I make far more putts when I believe I can do it than when I don't believe I can."

What are your targets? What are you planning to achieve with your life on this earth? We are amazed that most Christians, in general, and ministers, in particular, spend more time thinking about their goals and targets for a 7- to 14-day vacation, than they do for 70 to 80 years of their lives. In other words, they actually know where they're going to go before they depart for that vacation. They know how much it's going to cost. They know what they're going to do. They have taken the vacation vision and broken it down into goals or targets.

When we begin to set our goals, it is important that we take a God-sized vision and put it into bite-size pieces.

However, that same person, when it comes to 70 to 80 or 90 years of life, just believes it's all going to come together. They spend more time on a short-range goal than they do on a long-term goal. The reason why so many Christians do not finish the race before their life comes to a close is because they didn't begin with the end in mind in the first place.

In addition to targets, we need to think about time. Without the essence of time, it is impossible to set a personal goal, practical goal, or professional goal. When we begin to set our goals, it is important that we take a God-sized vision, and put it into bite-size pieces. And with each bite-size piece, there is a time element attached to it.

Just as there is winter, spring, summer, and fall, there are seasons in our lives. How we run our race later in our life is not the same way that we run a race earlier in our life.

Since we're on a journey that we've not been on before, it is going to take us longer than we think it's going to take. When we've been to a particular place multiple times, we don't even have to think about the turns on the road that we will make because we've been there many times before. But when we go to a place where we have never been before, it takes us longer, because the path is new. A good rule of thumb is to add 30 percent extra time to your goal setting.

When we get behind on our time, frustration and fatigue will settle in. Morale is low and tensions are high when deadlines are not met.

In addition to targets and time, we need to build in transitions. We need to think about the bridges of life that come our way. We need to think about the obstacles that no doubt will come, and we need a way to overcome them. Just like in air travel, from time to time we have to connect one airplane to another airplane to continue our journey. We also need to think of our goal setting and connection points. We then roll out our plan in phases with a successful process to go with them.

ACT ON THE PLAN

Now it is time to act on the plan. When we begin to start taking those first steps, no doubt there will be fear and trepidation in our minds, thinking, *What if this is the wrong plan? What if we didn't think of it deeply enough?* However, the plan that you now have is not in cement. We reserve the right to know more in the future than we do now. You will be updating your plan as you learn more.

Life is lived forward, but it is learned backward.

We have to move from procrastinating, processing, and planning to actually applying the plan. One of the major reasons people procrastinate is because they're concerned about whether or not they have enough money to fulfill their plans.

Many years ago, late one night, I (James) was complaining to the Lord, in the study of my home. At the time, we lived in

Springfield, Missouri. In the downstairs of our home was where I had my entire library, including my desk and credenza. While I was working that night, I was complaining out loud to the Lord. I said, "Lord, there seems to never be enough money. I've been working and serving in this ministry for so many years, and we ought to have more money than this."

When I became quiet, the Lord whispered to me, "People with vision never have enough money. And people without vision don't need much." What I learned from that experience was when God provides the vision, He can provide a stair-stepped plan to help you to get in the flow with the provision.

Whether I like it or not, I've come to learn that there is a tension between vision and provision. This leadership tension is found in the speed by which we apply the plan. If we slow it down, we will lose our momentum. If we go too fast, we could end up too far ahead of the provision that's needed to take care of it. Yet, we have to act on the plan. We cannot allow fear to rob us of the vision that the Lord has put in our hearts.

LOOK BACK AND REVIEW

Life is lived forward, but it is learned backward. While we activate the plan, there needs to be time when we reflect on what was successful and what was not; on what is effective and what is ineffective. When we look back and review, we will learn lessons that will help us to be better in our thinking, planning, and effectiveness. The overarching goal is to make fewer mistakes in the future than we did in the past.

Some leaders slow down at the end of each day and reflect on the meetings and phone calls that they had. They ask themselves, *What could've been done differently? Is there a better way to say it or write it? Where can I save more time?* Other leaders wait until the end of the week. And on Saturday they reflect on where they were effective and ineffective. They assess the meetings and phone calls so they can be more effective in the future than they were in the past.

SET NEW GOALS

Once we have looked back and reviewed, we are in a strong position to set new goals. Remember, our plan is a plan in process and progress. We consistently renew and revise the plan. It is never a finalized plan. So as the plan is updated, the goals must be updated also.

To set those new goals, we gather the facts, organize a plan, and then act on the plan. Over the decades of our respective journeys, we have had to adjust and update our plans and goals along the way. We have heard it said practice makes perfect. However, we suggest that it's the right practice that makes perfect. People don't practice tennis the way they practice soccer. It is the right practice that we want.

The future belongs to the finisher. And the level of our ministry's success will be based upon the leadership level that we can articulate, activate, and apply to our goals on a daily basis.

THE CONTEST BEFORE US

The world of our Lord was a world much like our own in that it made spectacles of athletic competitions and endeavors. In New Testament times, there were three great games: the Olympian games held in Athens, the Pythian games at Delphi, and the Isthmian games at Corinth. These games were staggered so that the wealthy could attend them all.

The games had boxing, wrestling, and the throwing of the javelin and the discus, as well as chariot races, which in time gave way to car races at the Indianapolis Speedway. They also had foot races, which is what the writer of Hebrews addresses.

> Therefore, since we have so great a cloud of witnesses surrounding us, let us also lay aside every encumbrance and the sin which so easily entangles us, and let us run with endurance the race that is set before us, fixing our eyes on Jesus, the author and perfecter of faith, who for the joy set before Him endured the cross, despising the shame, and has sat down at the right hand of the throne of God. For consider Him who has endured such

hostility by sinners against Himself, so that you will not grow weary and lose heart (Hebrews 12:1-3).

To be an athlete in the New Testament era was an incredible opportunity and privilege. The athletes who competed in these games were the most popular people in the country. Cicero complained that an athlete would often receive more accolades and praise than a general who was returning home from war.

The athletes competed in great amphitheaters larger than our stadiums. Some of the early theaters would be six times the size of one of our football stadiums.

At the end of the field would be an altar for a blood sacrifice to a pagan god. The athletes would bathe their hands in the blood of the animal, lift them to the heavens, and swear by the god they served that they would play by the rules, that their lives were pure, and that there was nothing against them that would keep them from running fairly. When the time came for the race to begin, the athletes would line up with every muscle stretched and every nerve at the ready.

Hebrews 12:1-3 is filled with some of the greatest truths to be found in the New Testament. The Hebrew writer is using a familiar figure to make a spiritual application. For the Ancient Romans, the Olympic Games were part of the grandeur of Ancient Greece and its Golden Age. The races and other sporting events were familiar to everyone.

Interestingly, the Word of God compares the Christian life to a course to be followed and a race to be won. Running this race according to Scripture implies intense determination. In a casual walk, one may look around and enjoy the scenery of a sunlit day, but in running a race, every muscle and nerve of the body is brought into full play with magnificent focus. The Christian life is not to be taken lightly but approached with great zeal and intentionality.

In the heavenly race that is set before us, there is a beginning and an end—a starting point and a glorious finish line—if we finish our race during our lifetime.

We are closer to the finish line than we have ever been.

In preparation for the ancient Olympic races, runners often practiced by attaching heavy weights to their bodies. For days before the race was undertaken, a runner would practice under the load brought to him by the weights he carried. However, once the race began, the weights came off so that they could be light-footed and run freely. A runner never ran the race encumbered by his heavy weights.

With the vivid picture of the Olympic runner in mind, we need to reflect on the contest before us.

In ancient days, the emperor would arrive at his plush box at the stadium where he would sit and look down at the games while thousands and thousands and thousands of people, tier upon tier upon tier, did the same. God has a race set for us; and just as the emperor was looking down at those runners so long ago, our Lord in heaven is watching us as we run our race.

In the spiritual realm, we are runners and there is a goal for each of us. However, we are not running against one another, for we are not in competition. Rather, we are on a pilgrimage with one another.

Our race is against sin, against self, and against life itself. The goal is not heaven, nor is salvation the reward at the end of the race. Salvation is what puts us in the race. It is not a reward for the righteous but a gift for the guilty. We must come to our Lord and trust Him and be born again to qualify to get into the race. "So then it does not depend on the man who wills or the man who runs, but on God who has mercy" (Romans 9:16). Thank God for His mercy that puts us in the race.

Our word for *race* is the Greek word *agon* from which we also get *agony*. The writer of Hebrews is talking about a marathon, a race that is grueling and agonizing—not a stroll. God has a race for each of us to run. There will be a level of agony in our achievements. Nothing ventured; nothing won!

We are closer to the finish line than we have ever been, and that reality creates for us many opportunities for thoughtful introspection. It seems that it was only days ago that we could hardly manage the thirst and ambition that came with being a young minister who thought he was ready for "the climb." Now, 45-plus years later, realizing that climbing only meant that the steps would all be uphill, my older self would like to tell the younger, "Son, just enjoy the journey."

The older we become, the more we realize that it is extremely important that life's ladder be leaning on the right wall of God-given, Christ-centered goals from the beginning, rather than a life filled with regret, remorse, fatigue, and failure. If you are under forty years old, slow down, and if necessary, stop. Think about the end in mind and ask yourself the question, *Is what I am living for worth Christ dying for?*

We are not letting ourselves wear the "old man" badge just yet, but we are chronologically advanced enough to know now what we wouldn't let anyone teach us in the beginning. In those days, we were too busy daydreaming about preaching at youth camps, camp meetings, and state, national, or international leadership meetings. Of course, we used to humbly camouflage all of that by saying, "I just want to be where I can reach the most people in the shortest amount of time." Truth is, we were too busy trying to get started with a bang to be very concerned about focusing on the finish.

Our friend, Dr. Leonard Sweet, has often said, "God wastes the energy on the young." He is not saying that energy is not needed. Rather, he is expressing that without mature wisdom combined with energy, young lives often believe that activity means accomplishment.

Thankfully, those attitudes were transformed to a more balanced view of life and ministry. We shudder to think where we would be now if those youthful attitudes had not changed. We know exactly when the change came. It came with being a husband, fathering children, leading churches, making disciples, and having our backside kicked by the boot of reality a few times. Sooner or later, if we are going to win the contest before us, we have to get our heads out of the clouds and our feet on the floor.

Somewhere in all of that refining process, we came to realize that the future belongs to the finisher.

Somewhere in all of that refining process, we came to realize that the future belongs to the finisher. Amid life's contests, we want to finish well and be well when we finish.

Indeed, something does come "after this."

- When there are no more stages to stand on and pulpits to stand behind;
- When there are no more planes to catch and places to go;
- When there are no more reserved parking spaces and front row seats;
- We want to be well. We want to stand in the winning circle, not the wishing circle. For us, the winning circle includes being well with our wives, our children, and grandchildren. Well enough to embrace every sunrise and welcome every sunset. Well enough to celebrate every success achieved by those who succeed us. Well enough to laugh at a humorous story and cry over a sad Hallmark movie at Christmastime. Well enough to pat future leaders on the back and really mean it when we say, "You're doing great. You are a far stronger person and leader than I have ever been."

- Well enough to keep doctors pleased that our weight is down, our blood pressure is perfect, and our arteries don't reflect all the bad food we've eaten in a lifetime. And most importantly, the contest before us means us being well in our souls.

To help achieve these incredible, faith-filled goals, we are doing our best to live by some guiding principles that better ensures a healthier finish.

EXCHANGE UNWORTHY GOALS WITH WORTHY GOALS

1. **Make your own personal discipleship happen every day.**
2. **Keep falling in love with your spouse.** Don't risk ruining your marriage to a competing affair with the church.
3. **Find a mentor and coach.** Sometimes they're the same and sometimes they're not. You haven't learned it all. Someone somewhere knows more about succeeding and even surviving in ministry than you do. The size of the ministry or the church doesn't matter.
4. **Make family your most important congregation.**
5. **Don't mistake perfectionism for excellence.** They're not the same. Perfectionism can lead to an early grave, while excellence honors the Lord.
6. **Don't lean your ladder against the wrong wall and just be at peace in the will of God wherever that may be.**

EXCHANGE UNCLEAR GOALS WITH CLEAR GOALS

1. **Find a confidant.** It may or may not be a mentor. You need someone you can talk to that won't be "talking you" to someone else when you're finished. That's why they're called "confidants." You can confide in them. Don't be reckless, however. Choose carefully and responsibly.

2. **Learn to successfully manage expectations.** Yours and the expectations of others as well.
3. **Remember, the church belongs to God and not you.**
4. **Accept that everyone doesn't like you or your preaching and that's okay.**
5. **Never be afraid to ask for help.**
6. **Remember, you are not defined by people's praise or criticism.**

EXCHANGE UNBALANCED GOALS WITH BALANCED GOALS

1. **Remember, the best thing you can do for the church is to take care of your own life: spirit, body, emotions, family, etc. Eat right and exercise daily.**
2. **Remember, people can disagree with you and still love you.**
3. **Remember, people will behave in ways that you must not take personally.**
4. **Remember, real success can't be judged only by your pulpit performance.**
5. **Remember, you should never apologize for resting and taking time away.**
6. **Don't ever stop learning.**
7. **Laugh often and be tender enough to cry when it helps.**
8. **Never allow the thought of failure to paralyze you.**

Here is how we run with the contest before us. Paul's words in 1 Corinthians 9:24-27 sum it up perfectly,

> "Do you not know that in a race all the runners run, but only one receives the prize? So run that you may obtain it. Every athlete exercises self-control in all things. They do it to receive a perishable wreath, but we an imperishable. So I do not run aimlessly; I do not box as one beating the

air. But I discipline my body and keep it under control, lest after preaching to others I myself should be disqualified" (ESV).

There is a **difference.** Paul says…all runners run, but only one receives the prize." If we are our best selves in Christ, we will win the prize.

There is a **discipline**. We read, "So run that you may obtain it." Every athlete exercises self-control in all things.

There is a **dividend**. We are not running "for a perishable wreath, but an imperishable one." It will be worth it all when we see Jesus!

There is a **direction**. Paul states, "I do not run aimlessly. I do not box as one beating the air." You are not to be a wondering generality, but a definite specific.

There is a **disqualification**. We must learn, "I discipline my body and keep it under control, lest after preaching to others I myself should be disqualified." We run with the rules in mind. Shortcuts do not pay off in the long run.

We have only one life to live, but that is enough when we apply our future to the finisher.

As we begin our heavenly race, we have the contest before us. As we run faithfully, time will work for us and not against us. We have only one life to live, but that is enough when we apply our future to the finisher.

2

THE CROWDS AROUND US

If we're going to move from the whining circle to the winning circle, we need the crowds around us.

There are those in the grandstand of glory to cheer you on. In Hebrews chapter 11, we have the heroes of the faith; a gallery of the great. There they are, all of the saints in heaven. They are what is called "a great cloud of witnesses." They are watching us. They are looking down upon us. Does that bother you that those up in heaven are watching you? Well, the Lord is watching you. They're made one with Him.

They are aware of us, just as those runners were running so long ago. Countless eager eyes were watching them, these heroes of the past. I wonder if there was a multitude watching them. What a great multitude is watching us. The crowds are cheering us on in the race. They are inspiring us to run our best. Remember, the future belongs to the finisher.

We submit that each of us needs to have 14 different kinds of faith-building people in our lives. These faith-building people will inspire us to go the distance, reevaluate when necessary, and pace the race until we have won it.

WORSHIPING FAITH: ABEL

We read in Hebrews 11:4: "By faith Abel offered to God a better sacrifice than Cain, through which he obtain the testimony that he was righteous, God testifying about his gifts, and through faith, though he is dead, he still speaks."

Cain's worship was based on works, while Abel's worship was based on faith. We need those kinds of people in our lives: those cheerleaders who inspire and illustrate before us. What worship is all about. When we worship right, we walk right. When our worship is flawed, then we will not finish our race.

The crowds are cheering us on in the race.
They are inspiring us to run at our best.

Abel and Cain represent two young men worshiping God. One is worshiping in spirit and truth; the other is worshiping by his own ingenuity. What was the way of Cain? The way of good works. It was salvation by his own effort. He was a tiller of the ground. God said, "By the sweat of your face you will eat bread"(Genesis 3:19).

Yet, in Jude 11, we read, "Woe to them! For they have gone the way of Cain." What is the way of Cain? It is to try to save ourselves by our own good works than by the grace of God. It represents culture rather than Calvary.

WITNESSING FAITH: ENOCH

In Hebrews chapter 11, we learn that Enoch walked with God and witnessed to his generation. He was known for his God-centered testimony. Enoch is the first one to prophesy the coming of the Lord in Judah. Once we have been saved in Christ, as we said earlier, we're in the race to win. Running the race doesn't save us, but salvation places us in the race. And once we are in this heavenly race, we are called to witness over the decades of our lives.

It is one thing for us to preach the gospel and lead a church or organization, but we are to be witnesses to this generation. As we know, Enoch did not see death, but he was raptured to be gone forever. And so it is with us. We are running a Christ-centered race, and our personal goal is to complete our God-given assignment before life comes to a close, or to be ready when we are raptured to be with the Lord. We need cheerleaders who challenge us to witness like never before.

WORKING FAITH: NOAH

In Hebrews 11:7 we read, "By faith, Noah, being warned by God about things not yet seen, in reverence prepared an ark for the salvation of his household, by which he condemned the world, and became an heir of the righteousness which is according to faith."

Notice carefully, "By faith, Noah...prepared an ark."

Noah's faith led him to do something. We know that faith without works is dead. We must learn to worship, walk, and work for God. No one could have said that he had faith; but had he not built the ark, he would've had no faith. He showed his faith through his works. Noah built the ark with concrete evidence of his faith. We cannot say we have faith in God if our faith in God is not enough faith to cause us to study the Bible, if our faith does not cause us to worship Him, if our faith is not enough faith to get us into the house of God, if our faith is not enough faith to get us into the baptistery, or if our faith is not enough faith to transform our lives!

As we have traveled and preached throughout the earth, we have seen, without exception, that where the church is flourishing is not only because of faith, but it's also because of faith that works. We have seen brothers and sisters who have worked hard and God has blessed their efforts. When you are selecting your closest friends in your life, be sure to have people around you who know how to work.

WALKING FAITH: ABRAHAM

Charles Haddon Spurgeon said, "Little faith will bring your soul to heaven, but great faith will bring heaven to your soul."

Abraham was an amazing man. His name is loved and revered by Jews and Christians alike. He is called "Abraham, who is the father of us all"(Romans 4:16).

There is no way to please God without faith; faith is the mark of a Christian leader.

In Hebrews 11:8 through 15, we read, "By faith, Abraham, when he was called, obeyed by going out to a place which he was to receive for inheritance; and he went out, not knowing where he was going."

We cannot emphasize enough the importance of faith. We're not talking about some incidental thing. "Without faith it is impossible to please Him" (Hebrews 11:6). If you please God, it doesn't matter whom you displease; and if you displease God, it doesn't matter whom you please. There is no way to please God without faith; faith is the mark of a Christian leader. We will never succeed in our ministries without believing in God.

Pause and ponder this: Abraham packs his bags and leaves familiar land to travel to a strange land. He leaves it all to go to a country he has never seen. God does not tell him where he's going, nor does He tell him how long it will take to get there. God does not tell him what he's going to do when he gets there or how long he's going to stay there. God just says, "Get up and go."

Over the years, each of us has had mentors who poured into our lives. We have made it a priority to spend just as much time listening if not more than talking. Listening is hard work and that is why so many failed to practice it. Rather than responding to a person's story with your own story, practice asking more questions about his or her story. We will be far wiser to borrow wisdom from others than to try to buy enough wisdom for the entirety of our heavenly race.

WAITING FAITH: SARAH

In Hebrews 11:11, we read, "By faith even Sarah herself received ability to conceive, even beyond the proper time of life, since she considered Him faithful,who had promised."

God gave Abraham a promise, but he took his eyes off God, as did Sarah. They did some terrible things that have impacted our world ever since. Even though they took their eyes of the Lord, eventually they got their hearts and lives back in step with God's promise. Fourteen years later, after Abraham and Hagar had a son named Ishmael, Sarah had a son named Isaac. God kept His promise!

From time to time, God will test our faith. A phase that cannot be tested is faith which cannot be trusted. The Bible speaks of the trial of our faith in 1 Peter 1:7. Our faith is going to come under attack. Never think there will be no heartaches or tears in life, but there will be problems.

As you seek to fulfill your God-given ministry, you will need to remember that you will need waiting faith. The Lord may put a dream or a vision in your heart in your early days, and it may not be completely fulfilled until your latter days. From the beginning until the end, you will need waiting faith. Waiting time is not a waste of time.

WILLING FAITH: ISAAC

"By faith Isaac blessed Jacob and Esau, even regarding things to come" (Hebrews 11:20).

As learned from Isaac, we have to step into the will of God, even though things at times can be quite confusing and complex in our spirits. There was no doubt a great confusion in Isaac's home, between Jacob and Esau. Yet, at the end of the day, the will of God was done in both of his sons.

We need individuals who can help us discern and decide what the Holy Spirit is whispering to us in each season of our lives.

Isaac came to realize and discover that a man is a fool to go against the will of God because it cannot be done. God's will cannot be stopped by any of our plans. God will let us have our share of our own free will, but under our free will is God's overriding will. We are to take the will of God and stand on it and love it because what God wants for us is what He would want for us if we had enough sense to want it.

All of us need to have people in the grandstands of our lives who will help us to find God's will. We need individuals who can help us discern and decide what the Holy Spirit is whispering to us in each season of our lives.

WRESTLING FAITH: JACOB

We read in Hebrews 11:21, "By faith Jacob, as he was dying, blessed each of the sons of Joseph, and worshiped, leaning on the top of his staff."

As you know, Jacob wrestled with the Lord all night long. We read in Genesis 32:24, "Then Jacob was left alone, and a man wrestled with him until daybreak. "He was in a wrestling match with the preincarnate Christ. Jesus Christ did come to wrestle with Jacob.

The point of the story is that the Lord began the wrestling match. God was trying to do something with Jacob, to deliver him from his self-sufficiency. They wrestled all night long. A mortal man in a wrestling match with Almighty God. When day was about to break, the Angel did something very significant. "When he saw that he had not prevailed against him, he touched the socket of his thigh; so, the socket of Jacob's thigh was dislocated while he wrestled with him. Then he said, 'Let me go, for the dawn is breaking.' But he said, 'I will not let you go unless you bless me'" (Genesis 32:25-26).

After the wrestling match was over, Jacob had a limp. He didn't walk like he used to walk. We need cheerleaders in our lives who are willing to wrestle with us regarding ideas, thoughts, and plans. We need intercessors in our lives who know how to bombard the gates of glory on our behalf. As you select your closest friends in your life, make sure you pull God-given prayer warriors close to you.

WISHING FAITH: JOSEPH

When you get where you are going, where will you be? You are going somewhere, but where are you headed? Are you satisfied with the direction of your life? Are you living, or are you merely existing? People without a dream exist; people with a vision take hold of life with both hands and move into it.

We read, "By faith Joseph, when he was dying, made mention of the exodus of the sons of Israel, and gave orders concerning his bones" (Hebrews 11:22). It was there that God smiled upon Joseph's life because of the faith he demonstrated before the Lord. The vision of Joseph's youth came to pass through the corridor of time, regardless of all the obstacles of the prison and palace.

Joseph possessed wishing faith. He was willing, from his youth, to expect God to use him in amazing ways. The God-given dream that had been placed in his heart renewed his spirit until one day what he saw in his heart he held in his hand.

We need risk-takers in our lives. We need fellow leaders who inspire us to take the next step up and the next step forward. Trust us when we say, the older you get, the temptation is to coast to the finish. However, no one will ever coast uphill; he or she will coast downhill. As we get older, we may not climb as fast, but we're still moving up and over to the finish line.

WISDOM FAITH: MOSES' PARENTS

Throughout the Word of God, in both the Old and New Testaments, we're exhorted to seek wisdom in our lives. There is a big difference between knowledge and wisdom. We read in Hebrews 11:23, "By faith Moses, when he was born, was hidden for three months by his parents, because they saw he was a beautiful child; and they were not afraid of the king's edict."

The parents of Moses were filled with wisdom. They knew that God's hand was upon their child, and they took the necessary faith-building steps for success. Even though they were living in an evil season on the Earth, they knew how to walk humbly, and uprightly before the Lord.

If you choose wisely to walk carefully with those who know more than you, and have lived longer than you, you will gain wisdom in your early years. If you approach life and ministry with a "know-it-all" attitude and disposition, you'll eventually go to the school of hard knocks and learn wisdom the hard way. Wise is the person who chooses to borrow wisdom, instead of always buying it at higher prices.

WEIGHING FAITH: MOSES

There will be times in ministry life when you are pressured on all sides. You'll be pressured financially, emotionally, narratively, mentally, and physically, all at the same time.

"By faith Moses, when he had grown up, refused to be called the son of Pharaoh's daughter, choosing rather to endure ill-treatment with the people of God than to enjoy the temporary pleasures of sin, considering the reproach of Christ greater riches than the treasures of Egypt; for he was looking to the reward" (Hebrews 11:24-26).

If you choose wisely to walk carefully with those who know more than you, and have lived longer than you, you will gain wisdom in your early years.

Notice these words: "considering the reproach of Christ greater riches than the treasures of Egypt; for he was looking to the reward." Moses was no fool; he did not live on the negative side of the ledger, but on the positive side.

We need to calculate the present versus the future. When life gets hard, we need to take the long look instead of the short look. Instead of looking for a way out, look for a way through to the other side. Moses had to decide. He had to decide whether he wanted the pleasures of sin, or the joy of Jesus; the riches of Egypt or the rewards of heaven. He had to exchange the temporary for the eternal.

We have watched ministers run for political office in their denomination. We have watched young men treat the local church as a stairstep to the next church. We caution you. Slow down, ponder, and weigh your choices carefully. Just as there are those in the grandstand's glory who weighed the tough decisions carefully in light of eternity, each of us needs to have weighing-faith individuals in our lives. Make a list of three or four such weighing-faith individuals in your life. Pray over them and determine that you want to be in the circle of their life.

WARRING FAITH: JOSHUA

Faith in God gets us out of trouble; also faith in God gets us into trouble. Sooner or later, we will face the walls of our personal Jericho, which tells us we will never possess our possessions and enter into all that God has for us.

"By faith the walls of Jericho fell down after they had been encircled for seven days" (Hebrews 11:30).

As ministers before Almighty God, we still face obstacles that need to be removed; and through the Lord Jesus Christ and by faith, we can be victorious. However, Satan will see to it that there are great obstacles that loom large and impossible between us and the plan and will of God for our lives. The Jericho for each of us will be different.

Over the years, we have been intentional in bringing courageous people into our lives. Just as faith is contagious, so is a courageous spirit. We have noticed that when we feel weak, we need people that we know are strong. When you are selecting the encouragers and cheerleaders in your life, look at what they have already accomplished. If they've not oversome huge obstacles in their lives, how are they going to be able to help you with yours? A picture of future success is found in the picture of past success. If a person has not overcome those obstacles in the past, it is doubtful they'll be able to coach you to overcome yours.

WELCOMING FAITH: RAHAB

We read in the Hall of Fame of Faith chapter, Hebrews 11, about a woman who went from the House of Shame to the Hall of Fame. Her name was Rahab. "By faith Rahab the harlot did not perish along with those who were disobedient, after she had welcomed the spies in peace" (Hebrews 11:31). This is the story of the transformation of a harlot whose name was Rahab and what the gospel did for her.

---

*A picture of future success is found
in the picture of past success.*

Her success was found in the fact that she simply opened the door of her heart and welcomed faith-filled people into her life. It all started there. We don't know much about her, but we do know that she didn't die with the others in Jericho. God spared her life because of her faith. We are confident that Rahab did not have huge faith, but God took the faith that she had and used her in a mighty way to bring the walls of Jericho down. It's not necessarily great faith in God that brings the walls down; it is faith in a great God who does it.

We encourage you to begin each morning with a welcoming heart for what the Lord wants to teach you each day. Additionally, you should desire to spend time with learners, with those who are still hungry for truth, wisdom, and knowledge. We enjoy being with people who are readers who can tell us about the top five books they read last year. We're never to pull our car over to the side on the highway of life and quit learning and growing.

WINNING FAITH: GIDEON, BARAK, SAMSON, JEPHTHAH, DAVID, SAMUEL, PROPHETS

We are sure you desire winning faith. We read of Gideon, Barak, Samson, Jephthah, David, Samuel, and the prophets, who "by faith, conquered kingdoms, performed acts of righteousness, obtained promises, shut the mouths of lions, quenched the power of fire, escaped the edge of the sword, from weakness were made strong, became mighty in war, put foreign armies to flight" (Hebrews 11:32-34).

You need people in your life who have paid the price of what it is to preach and teach the gospel in difficult places.

The stars in their courses will fight for you when you're in the will of God. Wise is the person who finds out which way God is going and follows Him. Unwise is the person who goes in the opposite direction. Simply get in step with the flow that the Lord has for you and He will help you to win in ministry and to finish your heavenly race.

We enjoy sitting down with the winners and talking about their life stories. We have always found that amid the winning stories there were battles they had to overcome. They were battles of beliefs in their minds and attacks of anxieties they had to overcome. It comes with the territory.

Make sure you have winners in the race with you, and the kind of winners that have your best interest in mind. You will need them from time to time to illustrate and inspire you to finish your race.

WANDERING FAITH: PERSECUTED AND MARTYRED

We read, "Others were tortured, not accepting their release, so that they might obtain a better resurrection; and others experienced mockings and scourgings, yes, also chains and imprisonment. They were stoned, they were sawn in two, they were tempted, they were put to death with the sword; they went about in sheepskins, in goatskins, being destitute, afflicted, ill-treated (men of whom the world was not worthy), wandering in deserts and mountains and caves and holes in the ground. And all these, having gained approval through their faith, did not receive what was promised" (Hebrews 11:35-39).

It is hard for us to comprehend the above words. Yet it is true; there are those in ministry who pay the ultimate sacrifice. In this instance, their faith got them into trouble and not out of trouble. You need people in your life who have paid the price of what it is to preach and teach the gospel in difficult places. We're not saying that you need to sit down with a martyr just before he or she dies. However, we are expressing that when we think we've got it hard, there's always someone else who has it harder than we do. We are grateful for the people in our lives that we know personally, who live in some of the most difficult places in this world. They are doing the work of God in the deserts, in caves of this generation.

We cannot stress enough that you will need as much relationship currency as possible to win your heavenly race. When relationship currency is properly stewarded, over time it will become relationship capital. When you have relationship capital, trust has been built and together you can build great Kingdom things that honor Christ. You will be where you are going to be five years from now based upon the crowds you have allowed to cheer you on in your heavenly race.

3

THE CONDITIONING WITHIN US

"Therefore, since we have so great a cloud of witnesses surrounding us, let us also lay aside every encumbrance [or weight in KJV] and the sin which so easily entangles [or besets] us, and let us run with endurance the race that is set before us" (Hebrews 12:1).

THINGS THAT SLOW US DOWN

In running a race, we cannot afford to let anything slow us down. There has to be discipline if we are going to run to win, but there are encumbrances that slow us down and sins that trip us up, either of which is bad. Some things are not necessarily bad in and of themselves. There is nothing wrong with an overcoat, but a runner would not be wise to wear one in a 100-yard dash. A runner strips down to the bare necessities (sometimes almost to the point of indecency). Nevertheless, we are to "lay aside every weight." Good things can be bad things if they keep us from the best things.

"All things are lawful unto me, but not all things are not expedient" (1 Corinthians 6:12, KJV). When we think of the word "expedient," we often think of an expedition, a journey undertaken by a group of people with a particular purpose. Paul is saying that if something does not help us go to the place we are supposed to go, it is wrong for us. There are certain things we have had to lay aside in our own particular life, not because they are bad in and of themselves but simply because they are excess baggage. We do not have time to read good books because we have not read the best ones. A good book may be considered recreational, and God does want us to have recreation; but so many times, we are simply wasting time. We must lay aside every weight—the good things that may be bad things if they keep us from the best things.

Good things become bad things when they keep us from the best things.

A good exercise would be to write down the things in our lives that would allow us to move faster down the track if we laid them aside—for example, the things we spend time, money, thought, and energy on. At our devotional time, we could pull the list out and pray over it.

Good things become bad things when they keep us from the best things. Life would be simpler if it were simply a choice between good and bad, but it is often a choice between good and best. "Let us lay aside every weight" and strip down to the bare necessities for your heavenly race.

We are called upon to lay aside every weight. We are not only to get rid of the sin but there are also weights that hinder our progress in the Christian life.

What are the weights of sin?

The spirit of discouragement is a weight. Nothing hinders a runner quite like a heavy heart. There is something about brooding over sorrow that paralyzes all spiritual power and activity. This could be what is wrong with many as it relates to their delayed victory. The heart freezes, the mind becomes dull, and the tongue stiffens, the hands and feet feel like lead, and life stagnates. If a minister steps into the pulpit with this weight upon his soul, he or she cannot be at their best for God. Despite the best efforts, the spirit will drop, and the congregation will go away empty and hungry. If we allow the spirit of gloom to possess us, we will become lifeless and useless. On the other hand, if we remain filled with light, love, and joy, there will be inspiration and life in our message.

Another weight is the spirit of criticism. There is no disposition of the soul that more quickly destroys the flavor of holy love than the spirit of criticism. The critical spirit eats away, like a burning acid, the very sweetness of a spiritual life. There is a mysterious quality of heart, gentleness, and mental and soul-sweetness in a truly crucified believer that cannot be defined. What is it? It is the breath of Jesus in the heart, the vapor from the river of life, the perfume of the Rose of Sharon, the sweetness of prayer, and the marrow in the bone of truth. One hour of critical thinking, or one severe utterance in a critical spirit, will strike through this inward purity and sweetness. This is a weight that must be laid aside, or we will come short of the purpose and plan of God.

Then, the spirit of fear is also a weight to one's soul. Fear clouds the mind and blurs vision until things are seen out of proportion. Fear was what led to Israel's defeat at Kadesh-Barnea. The people magnified their difficulties, talked about giants and walled cities until all they could see were towering obstacles. But Caleb said, "Give me this mountain!" If you magnify a fear, it will come upon you. This is what happened to Job.

If you entertain the thought of failure, you will fail. Fear a crowd and you will get stage fright. Fear people and you will fall into bondage. The fear of failure has hindered the work of many well-intentioned people for much too long. Fear is a weight that must be laid aside or it will clip our spiritual wings.

I (James) have a pastor-friend who has raised an incredible family and is no doubt a great husband. One weekend while I was ministering at his church, he shared with me that he loved baseball and that he had a baseball subscription so he could watch every game of his favorite team in a season. As I understand it, there are some 160 games per season! Just think about this for a moment. That is three weeks, per season, sitting, watching baseball. In ten years, that is more than six months! What could you do with an extra six months?

We (Tim and James) learned a long time ago that time is lost most times in the little things, not the big things. If you don't like where the train track is taking you, then be wise and don't get on the train.

We realize all of us have to work out our best plan to win in our heavenly race. We will say more about the individual race in a later chapter. For us, we decided years ago that when we travel, we would not check bags at the airport. What we take with us goes on the plane. And when we deplane, the same bags come off with us. We do not wait for checked bags in any airport because we choose to discipline ourselves before we leave for the next trip and to select just enough to keep us going without slowing us down. This might seem extreme to you, but can you imagine how much time we have saved? How must frustration we have not had because of lost bags? The journey is just sweeter when the load is not so heavy. Cast some things aside and you will experience a greater freedom to run the heavenly race.

THINGS THAT TRIP US UP

"Let us also lay aside every encumbrance and the sin which so easily entangles us" (Hebrews 12:1). There are sins that must be laid aside, sins that trip us up. We must deal with sin or sin will deal with us. Our "pet" sin is no friend. We must be ruthless with that sin and have NO MERCY on it for sin will have no mercy on us. It will entangle us, and we will fail to win the prize.

Simply put, besetting sin is an inbred sin that comes along with human nature. You may hear some people remark that their "besetting" sin is a temper out of control or unrestrained anger. Another may say that their besetting sin is a weakness toward certain temptations. However, besetting sin is the mother of all others. It is the sin of nature itself. In Hebrews 12:5, the writer calls this sin a "root of bitterness." A tree sprouts, grows, and is kept alive from the main tap root. Likewise, inbred sin is the taproot of all such sins as anger, malice, pride, jealousy, envy, and strife.

The lack of patience is what robs us of our victories, weakens our faith, clouds our vision, hinders our prayer life, and steals our unction and fire.

Inbred sin is that sin which causes one to be unkind and hurtful to others. It is responsible for all the division in the church and home life. The writer also speaks of this besetting sin as the "body of sin." This does not refer to the human body, but the fleshly principle or carnal mind. The "Old Man," as Paul called it, is deceitful and will play dead, only to rise and give trouble later. Inbred sin will not let go of its hold on our spiritual nature by mere hints or signs or resolutions.

Do not think you can shout it out or frighten it away by a few spiritual calisthenics. Carnality fastens its venomous fangs on the human soul, grips the very fiber of your being, and buries its claws in the innermost part of your moral nature. However, the good news is that through Christ, you may be made free from inbred sin.

Most assuredly, our race must be run with patience. Otherwise, we will miss the mark and will fail to reach the goal. Patience is necessary in our spiritual discipline, in the education of our higher character, in overcoming habits of sin, and in perfecting all the graces of divine life. Patience is the mother of those beautiful graces which adorn the sanctified life.

Perfect love is introduced to us as long-suffering and kind. The great work of the Holy Spirit is to cleanse the heart of all roots of bitterness and plant in us all the mind which was in Christ Jesus. The lack of patience is what robs us of our victories, weakens our faith, clouds our vision, hinders our prayer life, and steals our unction and fire.

God is looking for consistent ministers today who value relationships and fellowship with Him regardless of the challenges life brings to us.

Greater is he that can keep his will than he that can take a city. Greater is he that can let the other man have the last word than to have it himself. The greatest right you can have sometimes is not to claim your right at all. If I am to run this race with patience, then work should be done in me that will take out any eruptive-like nature and put within me a lamb-like spirit that will keep me calm and sweet under all circumstances.

When I (Tim) was serving as pastor, a young man walked into my office one day and said, "Pastor, I need to confess something to you."

Well, I sat up, paid attention, and braced myself for the worst. I didn't know what he was about to tell me, but as a pastor I had learned not to be surprised by much.

With all the seriousness he could muster, he announced, "I have finally determined what my problem is." He went on, "I am just real consistent at being inconsistent."

I was more stunned than amused. He had not only "nailed" his problem but also the same problem of a few others in the church as well. I didn't tell him, but after he left, I wondered if he had even indicted me. I spent some time asking myself, "Am I as faithful as I should be?"

If the future belongs to the finisher, we must be consistent regardless of the ups and downs of the track. I suppose most of us have "ups and downs." But how many people experience the "ins" and "outs" of Christian living? There is a huge difference between the two. Any child of God can have a difficult or a "down" day. But faithfulness means that we stay "in" the race, "in" the boat, and "in" the fight. God never gave us a "get out for a day" pass. We're "in" this for the duration. God is looking for consistent ministers today who value relationships and fellowship with Him regardless of the challenges life brings to us.

Are you a consistent intercessor?

Are you a regular worshipper?

Are you a faithful student?

How about a faithful giver to the cause of missions? Scripture teaches us that we are to be faithful unto death. Faithful to the faith, our family, and friends.

I was at a cemetery conducting a graveside service one day. As I walked away, I noticed someone had etched a previous statement on someone's headstone. It read,

"We always knew that we could depend on Him."

May that be said of us some day by our family and our friends, but most of all by Jesus Christ Himself.

Stephen Covey, the best-selling author of *The 7 Habits of Highly Effective People*, had written on his tombstone: To Live, To Love, To Learn & To Leave A Legacy.

To live—Enjoy

> To love—Embrace
> To learn—Educate
> To leave a legacy—Effective

Doesn't that say it all? While we live, let's enjoy life and laugh often. While we love, pull close our family, and do not let a day go by without saying, "I love you." While we learn, let's become stronger in our thinking capacity and become a thought leader. When we leave this earth, let's have the legs of legacy that keep walking long after we are breathing heavenly oxygen.

Those who finish would rather pay now and play later instead of playing now and paying later.

Someone has said, "I would rather burn out instead of rust out." Well, either way, you are out. The future belongs to the finisher, not the time waster or the sin embracer. Remember, it is the inside job that is the hardest. You will work harder on yourself than on anyone or anything else. Neither those who win nor those who lose enjoy the early training hours or the long hours of service in the week. The difference, however, between those who finish and those who don't is that the winner is willing to do the things that he/she does not enjoy, so they can enjoy the things they love later. They would rather pay now and play later instead of playing now and paying later.

What choice have you made? What kind of person do you wish to become? The stronger our soul becomes, the stronger our spiritual life will be. The Lord has selected you and has called you. Now you have the opportunity to set the pace for your fellow leaders and for your generation to go farther than any previous generation. We must lay aside every encumbrance and every weight that slows us down so we can run our heavenly race and cross the finish line victoriously!

4

THE COURSE BEFORE US

"Therefore, since we have so great a cloud of witnesses surrounding us, let us also lay aside every encumbrance and the sin which so easily entangles us, and let us run with endurance the race that is set before us" (Hebrews 12:1).

God has marked out a course for each of us to run from which we must never turn aside; however, each of our races is different. When the apostle Paul came to the end of his life, he said: "I have fought a good fight, I have finished my course" (2 Timothy 4:7). Paul's course took him to a Philippian jail where he had revival at midnight, to a Roman jail where he brought a slave to Christ, and to Caesar's prison where he set up a little piece of heaven right in the prison. Let us not complain about the race that is set before us, for God knows where we are and put us there or allowed us to be there. If we get off course, we will be disqualified.

The number one debilitating fear of people is "having lived a meaningless life." Do you know what your mission in life is?

How can you know if you are making progress unless you have a purpose? The purpose is the compass and the progress is the coordinates for your life and ministry. In a sense, you have an "ambidextrous calling." You will have to remain faithful to the Word of God and still minister "in an ever-changing world."

Whether you are just beginning an evangelistic ministry, pastoral ministry, or missionary career, or have been serving in ministry for some time, let us ask you one question: Why do you do what you do in the ministry? Is it simply to have a full calendar, money in the bank, or a national platform? Do you preach without purpose and minister without a mission? Let us never forget that the first and greatest evangelist of all time, Jesus Christ, could speak His mission in one clear, concise sentence: "I come that they might have life, and that they might have it more abundantly" (John 10:10). Even the early disciples knew what their mission from Christ was before they began their evangelistic ministry. Their mission was the Great Commission. Their goal was world evangelization. In ministry, you will either live your God-given mission, or you will live someone else's. You are either leading or being led. It is that simple.

Regardless of what form of ministry your life will embrace, you will greatly benefit from the principles in this chapter. This chapter will not teach you how to write a mission statement for your ministry, yet I encourage you to read books on the subject. This chapter will enlighten you as to the proper understanding of a ministry calling. This chapter serves as the bridge between the first century and the twenty-first century. With a proper understanding of this chapter, you should be able to know by the end your course to fulfill your calling. Your calling and your course go hand in hand.

How can you know that your life and ministry are your "God-given patent" for existence? There are many characteristics of a divine calling.

32

THE CHARACTERISTICS OF A MINISTRY CALLING

First, the God-given calling is **providential**. It has a sense of divine destiny about it. The call of the apostle Paul began before the creation of the world (Galatians 1:15). God knew Jeremiah before he was formed in the womb of this mother (Jeremiah 1:5). For evangelists to stay long term on the field, they must know without doubt that God has called them; otherwise, they will easily become frustrated with the stresses of itinerant ministry.

A divine sense of "who you are" will provide direction for "what you are to do" in ministry.

If young ministers do not know they are divinely called into full-time evangelism, they will eventually settle for "whining in evangelism" rather than "winning in evangelism." You will not be able to live with constant change unless there is a changeless core inside you. The key to the ability to change is a changeless sense of who you are, what you are about, and what you value. A divine sense of "who you are" will provide direction for "what you are to do" in ministry. If money was not an issue and time did not matter, what would you like to do for the rest of your life? Would you be willing to do it without charge?

Second, a ministry calling is **purposeful**. Abraham was called to be the "father of the faithful." Joseph was called to be a leader in Egypt during a time of famine. Moses was called to lead the Israelites out of Egyptian bondage. Joshua was called to lead his people into Canaan. The Old Testament prophets were called to proclaim the "Word of the Lord." Jesus was called to die for the sins of the world (John 3:16). Peter was called to be a fisher of men (Luke 5:10). Paul was called to preach the gospel to the Gentiles (Acts 9:15; cf. Galatians 3:15-16). When Christ calls individuals into ministry, He has a unique purpose for them in the church and the world. Why does your full-time ministry exist? Until you can answer that question adequately, you will not be clear in your decision-making, what you should do and should not do, and the direction in which you are going.

What are your roles and goals in ministry? Your roles provide your direction and your goals determine your destiny. For example, you have a role as a Christian, but your goal is to glorify Christ and enter heaven. If you are in Bible college, then you have the role of a student, and the goal, no doubt, is to graduate. You may have a role as a husband or wife, but your goal is to build a healthy marriage. These are three examples out of many roles and goals you may have for your life and ministry; and as can be seen from the Bible college example, roles, and goals will change throughout life.

What is your vision and mission for ministry? Your vision will flow out of your mission. Your mission is born from above while your vision is lived here below. Vision is cultivated by (1) looking above you (what does God expect of you?), (2) looking within you (what do you feel?), (3) looking behind you (what have you learned?), (4) looking around you (what is happening to others?), (5) looking ahead of you (what is the big picture?), and (6) looking beside you (what resources are available to you?). If your vision and mission are fuzzy in your mind, your morale will be low. All great leaders know where they are going and can persuade others to follow them.

Third, a full-time ministry calling is **personal**. Each of us is as unique in our calling as we are in being made in the image of God. (It would take an infinite number of human beings. St. Thomas Aquinas once wrote, "to mirror back the infinite facets of the Godhead. Each person reflects only a small—but beautiful—part of the whole"). Numerous Old Testament prophets (Moses, Isaiah, Jeremiah, and others) and New Testament apostles (Peter and Paul) were personally called to proclaim the Word of God. The evangelistic call is not just a profession but a divine act of God.

God has not called you to live someone else's mission and ministry. Many ministers live "unlived" lives before God. Your true identity or self-worth before God is much greater than your present level of ministry. God does not call an evangelist or a pastor to develop a ministry on the "proven personality" of someone else but on proven eternal principles. Be yourself. Whether you serve on a large staff, a lead pastor of a local church, or a full-time evangelist, God still has a unique, personal call for your life. The real test of a man or woman is not when he or she plays the role that he wants for himself or herself, but when he or she plays the role destiny has for him or her.

All great leaders know where they are going and can persuade others to follow them.

Fourth, our ministry call is also **practical**. For a calling to be right, it must fit our abilities. If you desire to serve as an evangelist, not everyone is psychologically able to travel for an extended number of years. One must have a changeless core to adapt spiritually, physically, and emotionally to a constantly changing environment. One must have a certain level of faith to believe God to provide financially on a weekly basis. It is recommended for someone interested in pursuing an evangelistic ministry to travel occasionally with a full-time evangelist to observe their lifestyle.

What are your gifts or talents? One of the reasons many of us don't recognize our gifts as gifts is because they seem so natural to us. Why do you suppose God gave those gifts to you? There is a God-given purpose for the unique gifts in your life. It is our responsibility to recognize them, use them, and expect fair wages for their use in our service to God (Matthew 20:1-13; 25:29). Your gifts and talents will help you to determine what kind of ministry you are called to. Do not mystify God's calling on your life. It is practical.

Fifth, the divine ministry call is **powerful**. A divine call provides both the passion for the necessary creativity and the power for the passion for the necessary creativity and the power for the renewed energies of the daily preaching grind. Facing hard tasks necessarily exacts dread. Indeed, there are times when we wish we did not have to face every burden our calling imposes on us. Still, finding ourselves where we are and with the responsibilities we bear, we know it is our duty—part of what we were meant to do—to soldier on. There is an odd satisfaction in bearing certain pains.

If your mission holds no personal passion, it is not your path.

The above observation easily applies to those who are called or set apart for full-time preaching ministry and pastoral ministry. If someone does not enjoy traveling, that individual is most likely not called to full-time itinerant ministry. If someone does not find renewed energy for the nightly preaching task, that individual needs to reconsider the pastoral calling. If one does not have deep compassion for the unsaved or unchurched, that individual's ministry calling is to be questioned. If a man or woman does not find inner fulfillment or a sense of purpose in missionary efforts, then maybe their unique calling is in another area of ministry.

If your mission holds no personal passion, it is not your path. Enthusiasm comes from the root words 'en' and 'theos'—which means 'in God.' What are you enthusiastic or 'in God' about? Do people have to prime your emotional pump, or does your passion for your mission get you up when everything else in life is down? Even though purpose is the motivation behind dynamic ministers, passion drives them to excellence when evangelizing the lost and equipping the saints.

Sixth, a ministry calling is **perplexing**. Even though the call of God is personal, sometimes it is hard for some people to discover it. Frequently, many false paths are taken before the satisfying path is at last uncovered. Experiments, painful setbacks, false hopes, discernment, prayer, and patience are often required before the light goes on.

Sometimes, several years of full-time ministry are required before individuals know for certain that the ministry calling rests upon their lives. I know of numerous instances where ministers have left the pastorate for an itinerant ministry after they discovered their effectiveness was on the road. I also know of evangelists who have left the evangelistic field to become pastors after they realized their calling was moving to *a* church and not *the* Church. Some know that their evangelistic calling is for a lifetime. They have served as the preacher-evangelist, the pioneer-evangelist, and the pastor-evangelist throughout their lives.

Are you seeking success or significance in evangelistic or pastoral ministry? There is a vast difference between these two concepts. Success is timely and dies when you die. Significance is timeless and lives on after you die. Soren Kierkegaard said, "The thing is to understand myself, to see what God really wishes me to do...to find the idea for which I can live and die." What is your all-encompassing goal in life? Is it to be an evangelist? Is it to be a pastor? It is to be a missionary?

THE CONFIRMATION OF A MINISTRY CALLING

A ministry leader is not only called by Christ to function in the body but should receive confirmation from the church. The ministry calling not only requires inward affirmation but also outward confirmation. In the New Testament era, Philip was well known and highly respected in his local church in Jerusalem. He was one of the original deacons chosen to serve the Greek widows (Acts 6). The local congregation also recognized that Philip was "filled with the Holy Spirit and wisdom" (Acts 6:3). It is important to note that before Philip was a leading evangelist among the Gentiles, he was recognized as a spiritual leader in his local church. The apostles were also supportive of Philip, the evangelist (Acts 8:14). Philip was sent out from the Jerusalem church to become an itinerant evangelist during the New Testament era. Since Christ has given the five-fold ministry gifts to the Church, churches need to realize that this person is needed for the ongoing work of effective ministry.

Christ provides not only the gift of the evangelist in the Church but also the grace to accomplish the intended task of evangelism.

Has your local church recognized your ministry gift or calling? Have other church leaders confirmed your calling? Are there open doors of ministry opportunities before you? Do your family members and peers see the God-given gifts in your life? Is there an inner witness in your heart regarding your ministry calling? Much soul-searching will help confirm an uncertain call.

THE CONTINUATION OF A MINISTRY CALLING

How can a pastor, evangelist, or missionary continue to function in the church for years to come? Is there a secret to building a significant ministry? What is one of the most important qualities of effective ministry? In Ephesians 4:7, Paul writes, "To each one of us grace was given according to the measure of Christ's gift." Christ gives the Christian leader "grace" to fulfill "the measure" of ministry. Each ministry gift in Ephesians 4:11 requires a certain level of grace to obtain the full measure of effective ministry. Christ provides not only the gift of the evangelist in the Church but also the grace to accomplish the intended task of evangelism.

Christ desires to provide both a compass and coordinates. The compass is designed to assist us with our purpose and coordinate with our progress. With both a compass and coordinates working in sync, we will be able to run our heavenly race and to bring our future into focus so that we may finish!

5

THE CONTINUATION BEFORE US

"Therefore, since we have so great a cloud of witnesses surrounding us, let us also lay aside every encumbrance and the sin which so easily entangles us, and let us **run with endurance**" (Hebrews 12:1). Endurance is the ability or strength to continue or last despite fatigue, stress, or other adverse conditions—to bear up under pressure. When I was in high school and college, I (James) ran a lot so I know what it is to run until my lungs are aflame and my muscles ache! It hurts! If we are looking for a cheap, easy, or lazy way to serve Jesus Christ, it does not exist.

Many people think they have done God a big favor when they come to church on Sunday morning and listen to a sermon. They call it their "service." Church is not a service; church is a filling station. Serving the Lord Jesus costs. We must pray over it, study over it, and weep over it. God does business with those who mean business. We will never, ever win a race unless we mean business.

While we may eventually leave some sermons unfinished, some songs unsung, some houses unbuilt, some flowers unplanted, or some needlework undone, we are immortal until our work on earth is done. We run with endurance and must not quit. No matter how far ahead we may be, we will lose the race if we quit. We must run with endurance in the race that is set before us.

WE NEED FUEL FOR THE JOURNEY

We read in Psalm 23:2-3, "He makes me lie down in green pastures; He restores my soul." Have you ever tried to go too far on too little? We all have.

I (Tim) have run out of gas too many times. Not because I didn't have any money in my pocket to buy some, nor was it the lack of gas stations along the road. There was always something within me that thought I could make it to the next stop, the next town, the next...whatever. Mark it off as a "man thing." I put it right up there without asking for directions.

The gauge says empty, but my stubbornness is full. The red light is on but so is my determination to make it just one more mile. Yes, there have been times when I caught a break and coasted downhill right into a neighborhood service station. There have also been times when the car sputtered, the systems failed, and I was stranded by the side of the road, embarrassed. Again, I tried to go too far on too little.

Too many attempt that in life. We bypassed the refueling opportunities thinking the last stop was good enough for our journey. The problem is a lot can happen between stops. To avoid being stranded, I've learned that I must heed the warning signs along the way. If we do not learn from past lessons, we are doomed to repeat them over again.

Here are a few warning signs:

Know Your Limits
The car manufacturer has estimated the distance the automobile will go on a full tank of gas. You must know your limits

as well. At some point, you have to "fill up." Additionally, the oil will go bad and it will need to be replenished or replaced. We are tempted to serve the Lord with yesterday's touch or anointing upon our lives. There is nothing worse than a half-filled Christian trying to overflow.

Read the Gauges

That red light means something, and you better not ignore it. It is coming from the knowledge that the frontal lobe of your brain can overheat. When you live in fear or flight mode for long periods, anxiety will build up in your mind.

How about your signals? Are they working properly? How's your temper been lately? Have you become easily agitated? You may have noticed that things that don't normally get under your skin have recently become irritating to you. That's a sign and you're trying to go too far on too little.

Are your lights working properly? Have you checked them? If not, when it becomes dark you will wish you had. The Lord wants to teach us in the day, so we can walk in the night.

Keep Up with Your Own Maintenance

Don't wait until you are forced to do it. When we purchase a car, we receive a service plan to help us maintain a long life for the automobile. But, if you ignore it, you will make your journey harder, or worse, wear out your car early.

Maintain a regular schedule of worship and prayer. Read God's Word and stay in good spiritual as well as physical condition. You'll go further and last longer. There are more miles to make, and you will travel every one of them after you've been refreshed in the Lord. The time taken to minister to yourself will be made up along the way in the progress you enjoy along the journey. And remember, the trip is worth your time.

Correcting Your Course

I've been on airplanes when the pilot had to do it. I've sailed on cruise ships when the captain thought it necessary. I've ridden on trains when the engineer had to decide to switch tracks. It's called navigating a "course correction."

Sometimes we catch ourselves going the wrong way. At first, it's not even detectable or noticed. It comes in the form of a casual drift that over time can take you out into the swift currents and dangerous depths of life's sea.

When Scripture instructs us to repent, it is saying that we must exit off the wrong road, turn around, and start traveling on the right road and in the right direction.

More than once, I've exited off the interstate to refuel my car then returned to the road to eventually discover that I was traveling back to where I had just come from. In my preoccupied state of mind, I failed to realize I was going in the opposite direction. Soon, I was looking for another ramp to take to correct my course.

The word, "repentance" means much more than being sorry or apologetic. It literally means to "turn around." When Scripture instructs us to repent, it is saying that we must exit off the wrong road, turn around, and start traveling on the right road and in the right direction. Jesus said, "There is a way that seems right unto man, but the end thereof is death." On another occasion, Jesus said, "Straight is the gate and narrow is the way that leads unto life, and few there be that find it."

Don't travel too far going the wrong way. What you need is a good GPS to help correct your course in life.

GPS? Absolutely. It stands for "Go Pray Some." Pray and repent and allow the Lord to correct your course today.

WE NEED TO KEEP ON KEEPING ON IN THE JOURNEY

Matthew 24:13, "He that shall endure until the end, the same shall be saved."

Victory is more than possible for the child of God. It is promised. Paul declared in Romans 8:37, "We are more than conquerors through Him that loved us." I must also join in with that same declaration of triumphant living.

Songwriter Dottie Rambo put it best in her song, "Too Much to Gain to Lose," when she wrote, "Defeat is one word I don't use." Is it possible to enjoy victorious living? Yes, but it requires trust in God, dependency on His Word, and an intentional strategy of the "dos and don'ts" of triumphant living.

Some time ago, I developed what I call my personal strategy for daily victory. Here is my personal strategy for victory. I hope it speaks to your life today.

1. Never determine your difficulties in light of your resources. There are no shortages in heaven. And, our God will supply all your needs according to His riches in glory.
2. Never make permanent decisions based on temporary circumstances. A wise leader takes the long look instead of the short look.
3. Never allow your memories to become bigger than your dreams. Dr. Tommy Barnett, the founder of Dream City Church and Dream Center International, has repeatedly said, "I only have one regret. I wish I had taken more risks."
4. Remember that delays are not denials. Don't forget you have an appointment with destiny.
5. Remember that there are some situations you're not meant to conquer but simply survive. Sometimes we

do walk through the valley of the shadow of death. The point is, we are walking through.

6. Don't break down before you break through. Take time for a walk in a quiet place. Breathe in and out five to ten times slowly, asking the Lord to renew His presence in your soul.

Remember, victory is yours today!

THE JOURNEY WILL USUALLY TAKE LONGER THAN WE THINK

Holding patterns are a frequent part of my travel routine and I don't like them. After long hours of bumpy skies, small seats, and gourmet pretzels, I just want to get home. While the shortest distance between two points has always been a straight line, I seldom travel that way. More often than not, I find myself going around in circles while others are landing and moving on with life.

God can give you something "good" now.
But waiting ultimately brings what is "better than good"
and ultimately what is "best."

Fundamental to our Christian walk is one's prayer life. Thankfully, we have found that God always answers prayer and sometimes He says, "Yes." Occasionally, He says, "No." Often, He says, "Wait."

We love the "yes" answers to prayer and we can tolerate the "no" moments, but we dislike the occasions when He says, "Wait." That's what He said to Mary and Martha when Lazarus grew sick and died. They had asked Him to come earlier and defeat sickness, but in His delay, He conquered death. You see, God can give you something "good" now. But waiting ultimately brings what is "better than good" and ultimately what is "best." A child of God can expect what is "exceedingly, abundantly, above all that you can ask or think according to the power that works within you."

Don't give up and don't give in to the temptation to yield to your weak and tired feelings.

God's delays are not denials. When He says "wait" He hasn't said "no," He's just saying, "Not yet." Like any plane in the sky, you must have enough fuel to maintain a holding pattern when you get in one. Our fuel is called faith. Circling the field requires more than flying on fumes.

HERE'S SOME FUEL FOR YOU

"They that wait upon the Lord shall renew their strength. They shall mount up with wings as eagles. They shall run and not be weary and walk and not faint" (Isaiah 40:31).

In the early 1900s, the World Heavy Weight Champion boxer, Gentleman Jim Corbett was quite the attraction. Sportswriters and news commentators were incessantly on his heels for an interview. Not always easy to pin down for a conversation, he was snagged one day by a reporter looking for a great insight into the mind of this great athlete. "What does it take to be the World Heavy Weight Champion?" the reporter asked. Everyone waited for Gentleman Jim's response.

"It takes...," Jim paused,

"It takes the willingness to fight one more round."

"Nothing profound or even difficult about that," you say.

Oh, really? Not unless you've been knocked senseless, and the world is spinning around you. Going one more round isn't hard unless your arms feel like they weigh a ton and your vision is blurred from the last barrage of punches you've endured. What's so hard about that?

You've been there. You know exactly what it's like. There's a price to pay when the words "I quit" are not allowed in your vocabulary. When everything around has sapped your strength, even those closest to you don't understand your tenacity. You keep fighting because you know the win is worth the pain.

Paul understood. That's why he said, "When you've done all you know to do to stand, keep standing." Don't give up and don't give in to the temptation to yield to your weak and tired feelings.

Is it possible? Absolutely! Here's how any champion keeps going:

Trust Your Trainer

No one appreciates process and preparation until it is needed. We always liked that scene in *The Karate Kid* when Mr. Miyagi had Daniel wax his car in continual circular motions for hours on end. Then he had him paint a fence in those vertical smooth strokes, moving the paintbrush up and down. Daniel didn't appreciate it at all until he got into a karate competition and all those moves he had learned in training came to be important in the fight. A true disciple will trust the wisdom of his Lord. Whatever He's using to teach you now will be important later.

Pace Instead of Race

Fight with the end in mind and then take the careful steps that get you there. Yours may be a 12-round fight. Use every one of them if necessary. Don't feel like you have to knock out your adversary in the first round. It is not a sin to rest in between rounds, so do it.

Be Consistent and Steady

I know very little about boxing but I've watched enough on TV to know that while a knockout punch gets the publicity, in reality, it is that steady and consistent left-hand jab that wears down the opponent. Consistency in prayer, reading your Bible, and attending worship at church are the best ways of all to ensure yourself of the ultimate victory.

Build Your Courage

Don't lose heart in the middle of your struggle because God is your strength and He is an ever-present help in the time of trouble. If God is for you, who can be against you? Greater is He that is in you than he that is in the world. David said, "When my enemies rose up against me, they stumbled and fell." Read it and be encouraged.

Listen for the Cheers of Your Fans

Paul said, "We are surrounded by a great cloud of witnesses." You can't imagine all the people that are in the stands cheering you on. Loved ones are there. Prophets of the Bible are there too. Most importantly your greatest fan of all, Jesus, is there. He'll even get in the ring with you if you'll ask Him. There are more for you and cheering you on than any who are against you. As a matter of fact, someone is shining your victory crown now.

Remember You Can't Lose

A poem written long ago sums it up well:

When things go wrong, as they sometimes will,
When the road you're trudging seems all uphill,
When the funds are low and the debts are high,
And you want to smile, but you have to sigh,
When care is pressing you down a bit,
Rest, if you must, but don't you quit.

Success is failure turned inside out—
The silver tint of the clouds of doubt,
And you never can tell how close you are,
It may be near when it seems so far,
So stick to the fight when you're hardest hit—
It's when things seem worst that you must not quit.
                    —"Keep Going" by Edgar A. Guest

6

THE COACH TO US

"Looking unto Jesus the author and finisher of our faith" (Hebrews 12:2, KJV). We look to Jesus because He is the Creator of our faith. It is not primarily great faith we need but faith in a great God and Savior. He is the author of our faith and the finisher or completer of our faith.

Salvation is a gift at the beginning of the race, and Jesus is the one who gives us the strength to run the race. Running the race does not save us. As stated earlier, salvation qualifies us for the race. Unfortunately, some start the race and never finish. They do not finish either because they quit due to backsliding or died before their race was complete. We are called to complete the race our Coach has marked out for us.

OUR MASTER AND MENTOR

Our relationship with this "Coach" is "looking unto Jesus"… not "looking at Jesus." What is the difference? Imagine someone in financial difficulty who is unable to pay their mortgage with the possibility that they might lose their home. However, a friend says, "Look to me." He does not mean, "Look at me." "Look to me" means "depend upon me. I will see you through; I will take care of you."

"Looking unto Jesus" is having faith in Jesus, not just having facts about Jesus. The Greek word that says "looking unto Jesus" is a word that means looking away from everything else and looking at something else. It is not looking at Jesus and other things. We must look away from everything else and put our eyes upon Jesus.

Salvation is a gift at the beginning of the race, and Jesus is the one who gives us the strength to run the race.

We must not put our eyes upon Satan for he will terrify us or entice us. We must not put our eyes upon the sins of those for whom Jesus died. We must get our eyes off of hypocrites and look to the Lord Jesus Christ. We must not put our eyes upon ourselves. So many people are guilty of morbid introspection. They open themselves up, pull their innards out, and stuff them back in again. That gets us nowhere. We must take our eyes off of ourselves and off of our sins, confess our sins and put them in the sea of God's forgetfulness, and look to the Lord Jesus Christ. We must quit saying, "What a fool I was!" and start saying, "What a fool I am for what a fool I was." We must get our eyes off all of that and put our eyes upon the Lord Jesus Christ.

The devil is diabolical and deceptive. He will get us to look at anything other than Jesus. He will even get us to look at our faith, wondering if it is strong enough. We must forget about our faith and look to Jesus. We must not put faith in faith; we must put faith in Jesus. The devil used to tell me, "Your faith is not good enough"; but I learned how to deal with him by saying, "That's right, but isn't Jesus wonderful?" Look away from everything else and look to the Lord Jesus Christ. He is the Coach; He is the Author of our faith and the Finisher of our faith.

The keynote of the entire passage lies in these words, "Looking unto Jesus." He is the commander and leader; the one who blazes the trail ahead of each runner. In the early days of American history, when the settlers were making their way westward to settle on the free grant reserve, the pioneer also known as the file leader went ahead on a swift horse, blazing the way through the forest, finding springs of water for the oncoming multitudes in their covered wagons.

Similarly, the world was like a moral forest. Humanity had lost its way when Jesus, our supreme leader, came and blazed the way through the wilderness and went all the way up to Calvary. There, He opened a highway of holiness and attached a light on Calvary's hill, which shines and burns brightly for everyone to find the way. While His pure body was still hanging on the cross, He descended to the region of darkness and walked up and hurled the prince of darkness into the ashes of hell and said, "I am He that was dead but I am alive forever more" (Revelation 1:18).

Then, on the Resurrection morning, He arose with a shout of victory, "Lift up your heads, O ye gates; and be ye lift up, ye everlasting doors." Jesus then ascended on high and took His place at the right hand of God. There He sits, undisturbed by the deeds of men and devils. No devil can tempt you; no disease can strike you without His permission.

It was while we were looking to Jesus that He gloriously saved us, sweetly pardoned us, and a peace like a river broke into our souls. Then, at the second look for cleansing, He sanctified us wholly and gave us the abiding Comforter who brought heaven into our souls. Again, we look to Jesus for perfect agreement with Him in all things.

In looking unto Jesus, we ask this question: What would He say, and what He would do under the circumstance which surrounds us? We need to look to Jesus for inward divine guidance. There are certain conditions upon which God promises to guide His children. One is that we acknowledge the Lord in all our ways. That means to put God first in business, ministry, pleasure, marriage, and all the details of life. The next is that we lean not on our own understanding, but on Christ, knowing that He will direct our paths.

OUR MEASUREMENT AND MOTIVATION

We read, ". . . the originator and perfecter of the faith, who for the joy set before Him endured the cross, despising the shame, and has sat down at the right hand of the throne of God. For consider Him who has endured such hostility by sinners against Himself, so that you will not grow weary and lose heart (Hebrews 12:2-3).

Our Coach knows what is best for us because He has gone before us and knows what we will face in our race.

Our Coach knows what is best for us because He has gone before us and knows what we will face in our race. The future belongs to the finisher. Let's look carefully at the success sequence.

Renewal
Jesus is the originator or pioneer. He was the first one to run this heavenly race and to finish it victoriously. He perfects our faith and helps us to get stronger over the years.

Rejoice
It is hard for us to comprehend the words, "who for the joy set before Him endured the cross, despising the shame . . ." How do joy, endured, and despising go together? When you know what the end result is of the race, joy overcomes the enduring required to finish the race.

Rest

We read, "and has sat down at the right hand of the throne of God." Just amazing! When our Coach completed His race, He sat down. However, there are times when He stands up, cheering His disciples to finish their race. When Stephen in Acts 8 was being stoned to death, He saw Jesus standing at the right hand of God, as if to say, "I honor you as you cross the finish line and take your rightful place in the grand stand of Glory."

As we run the race, we often remind ourselves that giants of the faith have already run before us. It is because of their pioneer spirit and faith that denominations and fellowship exist today. Someone had to go first and someone had to finish!

Reflect

Now, the Hebrew writer says, "For consider Him . . ." In the Greek text, this is a mathematical term. He is saying for you to carefully make a list of all the things that Christ, your Coach, went through to make you worthy to run the heavenly race. We challenge you to take out a pen and piece of paper and begin to write every sentence, every metaphor, every image that comes to mind as to what Christ endured for us.

After you have completed the list of what Christ has gone through for you, then make a list of all the things you have gone through or are going through in your life for Christ. Please note carefully that we did not say all the things you are going through. We said, all the things you are going through FOR Christ. Make a thorough list.

After you have completed both lists, then compare what Christ went through for you to what you have gone through for Him. When you compare the list, you will renew your mind and will not faint and quit. Christ "endured the hostility of sinners against Himself."

We are simply unable to fully grasp how a perfect Savior could go through the pain of the cross, the worst invention of a slow, painful death.

We hurt when we are whipped with the words of others; but Christ was whipped 39 times with the cat-o'-nine-tails.

We are angered when we are falsely accused, but Christ, the perfect Son of God, was falsely accused and did not even open His mouth.

When we see Christ sitting down at the right-hand throne of God, we know we'll make it and finish our race!

We are frustrated when we are not respected, but Christ was slapped, cursed, and beaten, and this was called "joy that was set before Him."

Do you want to win your race before your life comes to a close? Then stop measuring yourself to others. You are running to outdo someone else. You are on your track, your own course, marked out for you by God Himself. When competing against others for them to like us or to flatter us, we have lost sight of winning our race. Life is too short and the track too long to compare our lives to others. When we do, we will lose heart and quit. But when we see Christ sitting down at the right hand of the throne of God, we know we'll make it and finish our race!

The apostle Paul wrote, "This one thing I do, forgetting those things which are behind, I press toward the mark for the prize of the high calling in Christ Jesus" (Philippians 3:13-14).

Without great elaboration, this familiar verse from Paul's pen establishes three strong principles for running the heavenly race:

THE PRINCIPLE OF CONCENTRATION

This is "one" thing I do. Not two things or five or twenty, but one. How often do your priorities become shifted and jumbled around in a day's time? We all have "too many irons in the fire" and we lose concentration on maintaining focus on what's most important. Our most important priority in life must always be our relationship with the Lord Jesus. Everything else pales in comparison to Him. Jesus said, "Seek ye first the kingdom of God and His righteousness, then all these things shall be added unto you."

THE PRINCIPLE OF CANCELLATION

"Forgetting those things which are behind." There are some things in life that we just have to mark "canceled" on in big letters and put behind us: past hurts and grudges, disappointments, and failures. You must never allow anything to interrupt and stand between you and your relationship with the Savior.

THE PRINCIPLE OF CONTINUATION

"I press toward the mark." Don't quit. Keep pressing on.

My father said to me (Tim) on one occasion, "You can be impressive by how you start, but you'll be remembered by how you finish." I choose to live by the principle of continuation. I like a song I heard some time ago that says, "Quitting never crossed my mind." I like the song. I just wish I could say that I've lived up to it. I've thought about quitting a thousand times, but every time I do the principle of continuation kicks in and I remember Jesus walking the road to Calvary. There was no quitting in Him that day.

From time to time, in this heavenly race, you may grow weary in well doing. We sure have! Burnout and fatigue in ministry is very common and the statistics of those leaving the ministry are staggering. There is a battle for the mind that leads to the depletion of one's spirit and even to the weakness of one's body. Ultimately, the church and Kingdom of heaven suffer from the loss of good soldiers.

The demands of ministry and its accompanying pressures have worn many pastors completely down. In too many cases, the marriages and families of ministers have suffered more than most will ever admit. A sad reality is that church work and some churches can come close to killing pastors and leaders more than we like to think.

A sign out in front of one church perhaps said it best, "Don't let worry kill you. Let the church help." One pastor summed it up like this, "What once was a pure joy and a burning love to preach Jesus has become a treadmill of anxiety."

How does church work become so toxic and even deadly? Well, subtly and silently the shift begins to happen in the heart and one's identity moves from being loved and called by Christ to being admired and controlled by the church. A pastor is happy when church attendance is high but miserable when it's low. If the people are complimentary about our preaching, there is a sense of gratification and even fulfillment, but if the people criticize, it depresses and wounds a pastor deeply. The "anxiety of performance" presses into the point that it robs us of any peace at all.

Next, managing expectations quickly becomes impossible and the joy of ministry slowly leaks out of worn and cracked vessels that can't possibly hold any life-giving water to quench the thirst of needy church members, much less one's self. While we all love the church, we were not called to twist our personalities like a pretzel just to appease people's expectations.

No matter how long in the race we have been running or how many battles we have fought, we cannot fall back on experience. Some feel that they have done so much for the Lord that they can rely on past experiences, so they let up on prayer and become careless. They quit practicing self-denial until they lose the light out of their soul. This was the case with Samson and his backsliding. He began to depend upon his former strength until he went back on his Nazarite vows, which stood for separation from the world, and trifled with a woman's affection, and "He knew not that the Lord had departed from him" (Judges 16:20).

While we all love the church, we were not called to twist our personalities like a pretzel just to appease people's expectations.

Looking unto Jesus. The world is witnessing our race. Whenever we are successful and victorious, heaven rejoices, and hell mourns. Men may throw bouquets at us one day and stones the next, but we are to keep our eyes on Jesus, the author and perfecter of our faith.

By the time of the 1992 Barcelona Olympics, Derek Redmond, a British runner, had undergone five operations, including one on his Achilles tendon less than four months before the Games began.

In Barcelona, everything seemed to be coming together for Redmond at last. He was running well: he recorded the fastest time of the first round and he won his quarterfinal heat. As he settled into the blocks for the start of his semifinal race, Redmond's thoughts turned to his father, Jim, and the support he had always given Derek. Derek got off to a clean start and was running smoothly when about 150m into the race, his right hamstring muscle tore and he fell to the ground.

When he saw the stretcher-bearers rushing towards him, he knew he had to finish the race. Redmond jumped up and began hobbling forward despite the terrible pain he felt. His father ran down the steps in the grandstands, pushed through the police and security, ran out of the stands, and joined him on the track. Hand in hand, with Derek sobbing, they continued. Just before the finish, his father, let go of his son and Derek completed the course on his own, as the crowd of 65,000 gave him a standing ovation.

Redmond did not win the gold, silver, or bronze. In fact, he holds the worst time ever for a 400-meter sprint! Yet, the runners who got the gold, silver, and bronze are forgotten, but Derek Redmond's name lives on.

The future belongs to the finisher, and God will help you to finish.

We want to remind you, that when a race requires double or triple endurance and you have pain throughout your body, there are times, when your heavenly Father will come down the Grandstands of Glory, onto the track of your life and ministry, and will put His shoulder under your shoulder and will help you to finish your race! The future belongs to the finisher, and God will help you to finish.

THE CROWN FOR US

"Fixing our eyes on Jesus, the author and perfecter of faith, who for the joy set before Him endured the cross, despising the shame, and has sat down at the right hand of the throne of God" (Hebrews 12:2).

In the New Testament era, the name of an athlete who ran in the Olympic games and won would be proclaimed throughout the whole country. His family and kinsmen would be announced and honored. There would be a parade; the athlete's pathway would be scattered with flowers and he would be presented with costly gifts. If he was from Athens, his expenses would be paid for the rest of his life. Poets of national repute would write poems about him, and sculptors would make statues of him. The athlete who won would also win a crown. There was a crown for the Lord Jesus as well, and we are the prize that He ran for.

Every runner runs to win a prize: "Do you not know that those who run in a race all run, but only one receives the prize? Run in such a way that you may win" (1 Corinthians 9:24). Paul talked about his prize: "For who is our hope or joy or crown of exultation? Is it not even you, in the presence of our Lord Jesus at His coming?" (1 Thessalonians 2:19).

When we go to heaven, will we take anyone with us? Will we have a crown, a soul winner's crown? We must answer seriously, soberly, and somberly, for there will be a reward when we meet the Lord: "Behold, I am coming quickly, and My reward is with Me, to render to every man according to what he has done" (Revelation 22:12). We are in a race and must lay aside every weight and every sin that would trip us up.

There will be times when you may trip and fall, but you have to be motivated to get back up and continue in the race.

There will be times when you may trip and fall, but you have to be motivated to get back up and continue in the race. We would like to motivate those who have perhaps strayed from the course, fallen on the track, or dropped out of the race to make a brand-new resolve and get back in the race. There will be days that you may say to yourself, "What is the use of me trying anymore? I am not going to win." We can testify that there have been times when we messed up, did not get things right, or missed opportunities. Nevertheless, we have to get up and get going.

There are five heavenly crowns mentioned in the New Testament awarded to believers: the imperishable crown, the crown of rejoicing, the crown of righteousness, the crown of glory, and the crown of life. The Greek word translated "crown" is *stephanos* (the source for the name Stephen the martyr) and means "a badge of royalty, a prize in the public games or a symbol of honor generally." Used during the ancient Greek games, it referred to a wreath or garland of leaves placed on a victor's head as a reward for winning an athletic contest. As such, this word is used figuratively in the New Testament of the rewards of heaven God promises those who are faithful. Paul's passage in 1 Corinthians 9:24-25 best defines for us how these crowns are awarded.

THE IMPERISHABLE CROWN
(1 CORINTHIANS 9:24-25)

We read, "Do you not know that those who run in a race all run, but one receives the prize? Run in such a way that you may obtain it. And everyone who competes for the prize is temperate [disciplined] in all things. Now they do it to obtain a perishable crown, but we for an imperishable crown" (NKJV). All things on this earth are subject to decay and will perish. Everything is winding down to the grave. Jesus urges us to not store our treasures on earth "where moth and rust destroy, and where thieves break in and steal" (Matthew 6:19). When we look at a person's checkbook and calendar, we can write the priorities of his or her life. This is analogous to what Paul was saying about that wreath of leaves that was soon to turn brittle and fall apart. In this world, it decays and dies. But not so the heavenly crown; faithful endurance wins a heavenly reward which is "an inheritance incorruptible and undefiled and that does not fade away, reserved in heaven for you" (1 Peter 1:4).

THE CROWN OF REJOICING
(1 THESSALONIANS 2:19)

We read, "For what is our hope, or joy, or crown of rejoicing? Is it not even you in the presence of our Lord Jesus Christ at His coming?" The apostle Paul tells us in Philippians 4:4 to "rejoice always in the Lord" for all the bountiful blessings our gracious God has showered upon us. As Christians, we have more in this life to rejoice about than anyone else. Happiness comes from what happens, but true joy comes from Jesus. Luke tells us there is rejoicing even now in heaven (Luke 15:7). The crown of rejoicing will be our reward where "God will wipe away every tear . . . there shall be no more death, nor sorrow, nor crying. There will be no more heartaches, no more funeral services, no more hospital emergencies. There shall be no more pain, for the former things have passed away" (Revelation 21:4).

THE CROWN OF RIGHTEOUSNESS (2 TIMOTHY 4:8)

We read, "Finally, there is laid up for me the crown of righteousness, which the Lord, the righteous Judge, will give to me on that Day, and not to me only but also to all who have loved His appearing." When Paul says, "that Day," he is talking about the Judgment Seat of Christ. At the Judgment Seat of Christ, we will be judged based upon gold, silver, and precious stones versus wood, hay, and stubble. As we go through the test of fire on "that day," the gold, silver, and precious stones are refined, but the wood, hay, and stubble become the ashes of a wasted life. At the end of this life, we will not want to stand in the wishing circle, or the wasted circle, but in the winning circle!

We inherit this crown through the righteousness of Christ, which is what gives us a right to it, and without which it cannot be obtained. Because it is obtained and possessed righteously, and not by force and deceit as earthly crowns sometimes are, it is an everlasting crown, promised to all who love the Lord and eagerly wait for His return. Through our enduring discouragements, hardships, persecutions, sufferings, or even death, we know assuredly our reward is with Christ in eternity (Philippians 3:3:20). This crown is not for those who depend upon their sense of righteousness or their works. Such an attitude breeds only arrogance and pride, not a longing, a fervent desire to be with the Lord. We must always remember that the doorway of teachability swings on the hinges of humility.

THE CROWN OF GLORY (1 PETER 5:4)

We read, "And when the Chief Shepherd appears, you will receive the crown of glory that does not fade away." Though Peter is addressing the elders, we must also remember that the crown will be awarded to all those who long for or love His appearance. This word "glory" is an interesting word referring to the very nature of God and His actions. It entails His great splendor and brightness. Recall Stephen who, while being stoned to death, was able to look into the heavens and see the glory of God (Acts 7:55-56).

The crown is for all believers but is especially dear to those who endure suffering and bravely confront persecution for Jesus, even to the point of death.

This word also means that the praise and honor we bestow to God alone is due Him because of who He is (Isaiah 42:8, 48:11; Galatians 1:5). It also recognizes that believers are incredibly blessed to enter into the Kingdom, into the very likeness of Christ Himself. As Paul so eloquently put it, "For I consider that the sufferings of this present time are not worthy to be compared with the glory which shall be revealed in us" (Romans 8:18).

THE CROWN OF LIFE (REVELATION 2:10)

We read, "Do not fear any of those things which you are about to suffer. Indeed, the devil is about to throw some of you into prison, that you may be tested, and you will have tribulation in ten days. Be faithful until death, and I will give you the crown of life." This crown is for all believers but is especially dear to those who endure suffering and bravely confront persecution for Jesus, even to the point of death. In Scripture the word "life" is often used to show a relationship that is right with God. It was Jesus who said, "I have come that they may have life and that they may have it more abundantly" (John 10:10). Just as things such as air, food, and water are vital for our physical lives, Jesus provides us what is required for our spiritual lives. He is the One who provides "living water." He is the "bread of life" (John 4:10, 6:35). We know that our earthly lives will end. But we have the amazing promise that comes only to those who come to God through Jesus: "And this is the promise that He has promised us—eternal life" (1 John 2:25).

A lifetime of integrity prepares you for
a moment of temptation.

James tells us that this crown of life is for all those who love God (James 1:12). The question then is how do we demonstrate our love for God? The apostle John answers this for us: "For this is the love of God, that we keep His commandments. And His commandments are not burdensome" (1 John 5:3). As His children we must keep His commandments, obeying Him, always remaining faithful. So as we endure the inevitable trials, pains, heartaches, and tribulations—as long as we live—may we ever move forward, always "looking unto Jesus, the author and finisher of our faith" (Hebrews 12:2) and receive the crown of life that will not pass away.

Do you want to stand in the wishing circle, wasted circle, or the winning circle? The wishing circle is filled with countless numbers of Christians, who say, "I wish I had done this. I wish I could do it all over again. I wish I had not wasted so much time on small things"

The wasted circle is filled with people who came to the corner of temptation and desire and made the wrong turn down the road of lust, pride, and greed.

When we think about the winning circle, immediately, think of Joseph. We are reminded of Joseph's race he had to run in Genesis chapters 38 through 50. His race was filled with complexity, corruption, and cost. Joseph understood the true worth of a coat versus a testimony. Joseph had both, and he knew the value of each. One could be replaced with a few dollars but the other was irreplaceable at any price. One was made with a needle and thread over a few days but the other was made with good choices, patient responses, and wise decisions made over years of living day by day.

The story of Joseph beats anything currently airing on television or sitting on a bookshelf. It's full of drama, intrigue, and mystery. It appears to lack comedy throughout most of the story except for what snickering Satan must have been doing. Be assured, however, without gloating and exercising any pride, Joseph got the last laugh. And those who laugh last, laugh the longest.

He had already lived a difficult life.

He was hated by his brothers.

He was stripped of his coat of many colors.

He was thrown in a pit and forsaken.

He was sold into slavery.

He was slandered and falsely accused.

He was thought of least by those he had helped most.

When it couldn't get any worse, a woman tried to seduce him, told a lie about him, and laughed when her husband had him thrown in prison. Scripture records that one day as Joseph walked near Potiphar's wife, she reached out and grasped his shoulder. In that instant, Joseph was immediately placed in a battle between right and wrong, but he never struggled with his decision. Almost instinctively, he simply ran away. Others would have taken a long time to decide.

There is a powerful reason the apostle Paul said "Flee youthful lusts" (2 Timothy 2:22).

Now read these next lines very carefully. Some people, when confronted with temptation ask themselves these two questions: 1) "What's right?"; and 2) "Now what am I going to do?"

Joseph didn't have to ask either question. He had a heart for God, and nothing was worth offending Him and losing his testimony with others.

A lifetime of integrity prepares you for a moment of temptation. A shoddy life of comprise leaves one vulnerable and open to the enemy's sinister plan to bring you down. Joseph's decision was made long before Potiphar's wife ever touched his shoulder. From his youth, he had made good decisions, one right after the other, and with each one, his character had become rock solid.

While none of us are "above" temptation, some are more prepared than others, and it comes down to one word: "Faithfulness."

PICTURE THIS IMAGE...

Potiphar's wife stands in the hallway grasping an empty coat. That's all she had to show for her wicked attempt to destroy a good man's name. Though for a while she used it as trumped-up evidence, Joseph's good character eventually vindicated his reputation.

If you are going to run your heavenly race and win the crown, you will have to ask yourself the question, "What's my choice today? Tomorrow? In the future?"

Remember, you can always get another coat. The future belongs to the finisher.

Do you want to take hold of your future, finish victorious, and receive your crown?

Here are the rules of the road:

Read Your Map Before You Leave Home

Even though we live in an age of sophisticated technology, a wise servant begins with the end in mind. You need to study the map before you leave home. Each morning, no matter how long we have been in ministry, we need to study the Word of God and devote ourselves to a quiet time of prayer.

Stop at Red Lights

As we travel through life and ministry, there are times we will come to a red light. When the light is red, we stop. When we come to the red light of temptation, we stop. We saturate the place with our absence and get out as fast as possible. As we said earlier, we can buy a new coat; but our character is priceless.

Yield the Right-of-way to Others

We need to respect authority. When we are traveling, there are times we come to a yield sign. When we come to the yield sign, we slow down and respect the authority of the ongoing traffic. There are times in every field of ministry that others must go ahead of us. We urge you not to push your way to the front of the line. One of the main reasons, Joseph did not sin is because he highly regarded and respected Potiphar and his house.

Go at Green Lights

When the light turns green, then go. When God changes the light to green, when He gives you a green light in your spirit and soul, then get moving forward to fulfill His will.

If you follow the rules of the road and stay faithful to your calling, you will possess your imperishable crown, the crown of rejoicing, the crown of righteousness, the crown of glory, and the crown of life.

CONCLUSION

In the New Testament era, the Olympic Games included track and field events—the main event being running. Paul described the Christian life as a race—a race to become what God wants us to be. In that context, it helps us understand what seems to be a contradiction between Philippians 3:12 and 3:15.

Verse 12 states, "Not that I have already obtained it or have already become perfect." Verse 15 states, *"Let us therefore, as many as are perfect."* We must note that Paul was not talking about sinless perfection. The contextual idea is not our being perfect in terms of being sinless; rather, he was writing about maturity, our progress in the Christian life, and talking about relative perfection, not ultimate perfection.

An example would be a child growing up and going through the various stages of development. At age 12, we would say of her, "She is a perfect 12-year-old." That does not mean she is a grown woman, but at that stage in her development, she is a perfect 12-year-old girl.

Consider a man who is running the mile. He clocks off the first lap of the four laps. Those timing him say he had a perfect first lap. That does not mean the race is over or that he might not improve and make additional progress. It means that at that stage in the race, he is exactly where he needs to be, which is what Paul was saying. We are in a race. We are in the race of the Christian life, a race toward maturity.

We must be ready to start the race; it begins today. We are at the starting line, the gun fires, and the race begins. We are to follow the progress of the Christian race.

FINDING CHRIST IN THE HEAVENLY RACE

Paul wrote, "Not as though I had already attained, either were already perfect: but I follow after, if that I may apprehend that for which also I am apprehended of Christ Jesus" (Philippians 3:12, KJV). Paul was talking about the start of the race.

Apprehend

The word "apprehend" means "to lay hold of." Paul was talking about his experience of salvation—when the race began in his life. This may sound trite, but it is essential: We cannot run the race until we begin the race. There must be a time when we get in position on the starting block to be ready when the gun fires to start the race. Paul's race began on the Damascus Road when the Lord Jesus Christ "apprehended" him or laid hold of him and his life.

The same thing is true for every believer. If we have truly been saved and know Christ as our Savior, there was a time when Jesus laid hold of our lives. It might have been in a church service, while watching television, or at our bedside. Jesus apprehended us and laid hold of our life. Take hold of the eternal life to which you were called (1 Timothy 6:12). Jesus lays hold of us in grace, and we lay hold of Him by faith.

That I may apprehend that . . . The gun has been fired. The heavenly race has begun.

Apprehensive

Paul then says, *I am apprehended of Christ Jesus.* He has not yet arrived; he has not yet attained. He is apprehensive. "I have not yet become everything Jesus has saved me to become."

A first grader went to school on the first day of school and came home on Friday and announced to his mom, "I'm not going back to school next week." She asked, "Why not?" He said, "Because they can't teach me any more."

Sometimes Christians think that way. They believe they have arrived in the Christian life, but we never arrive in the Christian life. We do not know everything there is to know about the Bible. We have not grown the way God wants us to grow in the Christian life, so we make up our minds that we have not yet arrived, that we have not yet apprehended, that we are not yet everything God wants us to be.

Alfred Lord Tennyson was one of the greatest poets of all time. His poem, "In Memoriam," is one of the greatest ever written, and he spent 17 years writing it and would likely have rewritten portions of the poem numerous times. He never arrived; he never reached perfection.

We must remember that there is a heavenly race yet to be run.

FOLLOWING CHRIST IN THE HEAVENLY RACE

Perhaps we are an athlete. Perhaps we are a runner or a jogger. Paul uses a picture of running the race and how it applies to making progress in the Christian life. The gun has been fired. The heavenly race has begun. We are now running the race.

Concentration on the Present

Paul gave us several crucial elements of running the race. "I do not regard myself as having laid hold of it yet; but **one thing** I do" (Philippians 3:13, emphasis added). Paul was concentrating on the present.

The Bible uses the phrase **one thing** numerous times:

- The blind man said of Jesus when He healed him, "Whether He is a sinner, I do not know; **one thing** I do know, that though I was blind, now I see" (John 9:25, emphasis added).
- "**One thing** I have asked from the Lord, that I shall seek: That I may dwell in the house of the Lord all the days of my life, To behold the beauty of the Lord And to meditate in His temple" (Psalm 27:4, emphasis added).
- Looking at the rich young ruler, Jesus felt a love for him and said to him, "**One thing** you lack: go and sell all you possess and give to the poor, and you will have treasure in heaven; and come, follow Me" (Mark 10:21, emphasis added).
- Jesus said to Martha, "Only **one thing** is necessary, for Mary has chosen the good part, which shall not be taken away from her" (Luke 10:42, emphasis added).

Paul picked up the terminology of one thing and said that he was putting total concentration on the heavenly race—a concentration on the present.

There is tremendous power in concentration. One of the things that makes an electric drill so powerful is the tremendous concentration of power at one point. Consider the concentration of a great concert pianist or a field goal specialist on a football team. Both concentrate their efforts and work tirelessly on doing that one thing.

Paul told us we need to concentrate our total attention on the assignment of running the heavenly race for the Lord Jesus Christ. We are not a wandering generality but a definite specific! There are too many Christians who do not say, "But one thing I do," but say instead, "These 40 things I dabble in." "Teach me Your way, O Lord; I will walk in Your truth; Unite my heart to fear Your name" (Psalm 86:11).

As Christians, are we focused? Are we in a zone about our Christian life? How is it that Christians think they can grow and mature in their Christian life and not have total concentration? We must concentrate on the present and be able to say, "But one thing I do."

If we want to be a victorious Christian leader who excels, then we must be like the runner: "But one thing I do." We must get our minds on what we are doing.

Obliteration of the Past

We must also forget what lies behind (Philippians 3:13). There must be an obliteration of the past.

God said, "I will forgive their iniquity, and their sin I will remember no more" (Jeremiah 31:34); and "I will be merciful to their iniquities, And I will remember their sins no more" (Hebrews 8:12). These verses do not mean that God has some kind of divine amnesia and does not remember our sin.

Some ministers never make progress in their Christian service because they are dwelling on the past.

Paul was not saying that we will not have any memories of the past but that we are not to allow the past to influence or affect us. We are not to let the past keep us from winning the race. We are not to run looking back over our shoulders. Runners who have competed in races know that one of the basic rules of winning the race is never to look back over their shoulders.

Some ministers never make progress in their Christian service because they are dwelling on the past. It has been said that memory is a nursery where children, now grown old, play with broken toys. The load of tomorrow added to that of yesterday and carried today makes the strongest falter.

One of the things that we should forget is our past sins. If we have confessed them to God, He has forgiven us. We must accept God's forgiveness because our sins are buried in the depths of the sea (Micah 7:19).

One of the things we should forget is our past failures. There is no need to cry over spilled milk. All have failed. Thomas Edison, the great inventor, conducted thousands of experiments that failed before he invented the electric light bulb. We must build on our mistakes, not dwell on them.

One of the things we should forget is our past grievances.

One of the things we should forget is our past successes. It is so easy for a church to dwell on the past and say, "We used to do it this way," or "We used to do it that way," or "I liked it the way it used to be." The past is gone forever. While we thank God for the successes and blessings of the past, we are living in the present.

One of the things we should forget is our past grievances. "They did me wrong, and I was counting on them." Many ministers have past grievances that eat their hearts out, wreck their Christian life, and spoil their testimony. They become bitter, grumpy, complaining believers because they dwell on past grievances. Joseph had an opportunity to be like that with his own brothers; but he said instead, "You meant evil against me, but God meant it for good" (Genesis 50:20). God is in charge and knows what He is doing in our life.

Pressing Toward the Mark

The runner is on the move: But one thing I do—is concentrate on the present; forgetting what lies behind—obliteration of the past; reaching forward to what lies ahead—and total concentration on the future.

Every muscle in the runner's body is stretching and straining. His heart is pumping blood furiously. His lungs are taking in great chunks of oxygen. His feet are pounding the surface of the track. He is stretched out—reaching toward those things that are before him.

Paul was teaching us how to live the Christian life—looking toward the future. We should live the Christian life thinking about what we can do for Jesus Christ tomorrow and about what God is going to do in our lives today. It is not the time to give up in the race. It is time to keep on stretching to the finish line.

FINISHING FOR CHRIST IN THE HEAVENLY RACE

The first picture is starting the race. The second picture is running the race. The third picture is winning the race.

"I press on toward the goal for the prize" (Philippians 3:14). Paul was talking about winning the race—the mark to be reached. He was in the home stretch and saw the tape of the finish line ahead.

The Mark to Reach

"Fixing our eyes on Jesus, the author and perfecter of faith" (Hebrews 12:2). Jesus starts us in the race and is the finisher of our faith. Jesus is at the starting line to get us going and at the finish line to welcome us when we get there. The goals of the race are to be like Jesus and to finish His assignment He has given to us. The purpose of the Christian life is to be like Jesus Christ.

"I press on toward the goal for the prize of the upward call of God in Christ Jesus" (Philippians 3:14). Paul is running now towards the tape.

The Medal to Reward

When the runner turns the last curve and heads into the final stretch and hits the tape, he knows it is time for the reward. There is thunderous applause from the people in the stands.

In Paul's time, an official would come to the runner and say, "You've been called up." The successful, victorious athlete would go to the emperor's box; and the emperor would congratulate the successful runner and award him the prize—the emblem of his victory.

An Olympic victor who was a citizen of Athens in the year 600 BC could expect to receive a cash award of 500 drachmai, a literal fortune. From an Athenian inscription of the fifth century BC, Olympic victors received a free meal in the city hall every day for the rest of their lives, a kind of early pension plan. Later, in the Hellenistic and Roman periods, pensions for athletes became more formalized and could be bought and sold.

Jesus is at the starting line to get us going and at the finish line to welcome us when we get there.

"Do you not know that those who run in a race all run, but only one receives the prize? Run in such a way that you may win" (1 Corinthians 9:24). In a race, one person wins the prize; but as Christians, everyone can win the prize. Some day we will all "hit the tape," and we will say, "There is laid up for me the crown of righteousness, which the Lord, the righteous Judge, will award to me on that day" (2 Timothy 4:8). For those who are faithful and finish, God will give a medal, and perhaps it will be engraved with "Well done" for "Well done, good and faithful servant" (Matthew 25:23, NIV).

In 2 Timothy, the last book of which we have any record that Paul wrote, he said, "I have fought the good fight, I have finished the course, I have kept the faith; in the future, there is laid up for me the crown of righteousness, which the Lord, the righteous Judge, will award to me on that day; and not only to me, but also to all who have loved His appearing" (2 Timothy 4:7-8).

There came a day when the Roman guards of the Mamertime Prison took Paul across the highway to the guillotine and placed his head on the chopping block. The blade came down, severing his head from his body, and his head rolled into the dust. Someone may have said, "Poor Paul. He just bit the dust." However, that was not the case. Paul "hit the tape"; and Jesus said, "Well done, Paul. You've run a good race. Here's your heavenly prize."

Some die unknown and unmourned on obscure mission fields, and some may think, *That poor missionary bit the dust.* No, that missionary "hit the tape."

Not far from the Matterhorn in Switzerland is a cemetery where many of the great mountain climbers are buried. On one of the tombstones is written, "He died climbing." What an epitaph!

"Lord, lift me up and let me stand, By faith, on heaven's tableland, A higher plane than I have found; Lord, plant my feet on higher ground" ("Higher Ground," Johnson Oatman, Jr., 1898).

Running a marathon represents one of the highest measurements of human strength and endurance. It is a 26.2-mile run that was inspired by the legend of an ancient Greek messenger who ran from a city known as Marathon all the way to Athens to bring news of an important Greek victory over the Persian army in 490 BC. According to the legend, after the runner completed the journey and delivered his message, he collapsed and died. To commemorate this dramatic run, the Olympics established this race which has remained the "gold standard" for runners. One of the holy grails of marathon runners is to break the 2-hour mark. The current official fastest time is 2 hours, 1 minute, and 39 seconds held by Kenyan runner Eliud Kipchoge. (Kipchoge actually broke the 2-hour length in Vienna in 2019 but it was not an official race).

The 1968 Summer Olympics took place in Mexico City. One of the highlights of the Summer Olympics is, of course, the Marathon. If you had been in the stands that day at the end of the race you would have seen three men standing on the victory platform. It was one of those truly multicultural moments which made the Olympics so special. On the platform was Mamo Wolde from Ethiopia, receiving the gold medal; Kenji Kimihara, from Japan, receiving the silver medal; and Mike Ryan, from New Zealand receiving the bronze medal. Three men from three different continents racing in a fourth continent for this highest prize. But, as thrilling as that may have been to see, that was not the real story of the 1968 Marathon. Let me tell you another story of the 1968 Marathon which took place on that day.

Our eternal Father did not set us apart and call us into full-time ministry for us to begin a race and not complete it.

Long after the Ethiopian national anthem was sung, and after all the medals had been awarded, and even after most of the audience in the stands had left the stadium, John Stephen Ahkwari, the Marathon runner from Tanzania, entered the stadium. At the 19-kilometer mark, he experienced cramping due to the high altitude. Back in Tanzania, he had not been able to train for the high altitude of Mexico City. The cramping caused him to swerve unexpectedly and he was hit by another runner. John fell down and badly injured his knee, dislocating it, and his shoulder was badly wounded from the fall. But he got up and kept running, even though in pain and limping as he ran. He entered the stadium a full hour after the victors had entered and he was the official "last place" finisher of the race. Eighteen racers had quit that day, so he was 57th among 75 who started. People were amazed to see him enter the stadium in such obvious pain. Reporters and cameras ran to the scene as he limped across the finish line. They asked why he had continued running after such an injury. He replied, "My country did not send me 5,000 miles to start the race; they sent me 5,000 miles to finish the race."

We have a heavenly race to run. Our eternal Father did not set us apart and call us into full-time ministry for us to begin a race and not complete it. The future belongs to the finisher, regardless if it is a goal, a sermon, a church plant, or a missionary journey. If the Lord has called us to a particular course or track to run, then there is no better time to begin than today, no greater season than now, and no greater generation to impact for Christ than now. This is your greatest moment! Seize it!

Appendix 1

HOW CAN I KNOW GOD CALLED ME TO PREACH?

Martin Lloyd Jones, the renowned pastor of Westminster Chapel from 1938 to 1968 in London, England, stated, "If there is anything else a man can do other than preach, he ought to do it. The pulpit is no place for him."

The ministry is not merely something an individual can do, but what he or she must do. A God-called person would rather die than live without preaching. Charles H. Spurgeon, pastor of Metropolitan Tabernacle, said, "If you can do anything else, do it. If you can stay out of the ministry, stay out of the ministry." In other words, only those who believe they are chosen by God for the pulpit should proceed in undertaking this sacred task.

"Preachers are born, not made. This is an absolute. You will never teach a man to be a preacher if he is not already one," stated Lloyd Jones. A person is called, chosen, and then commissioned.

What constitutes this call to preach? How can you know that you are called to the "sacred desk" to preaching the living Word of God? We believe there are seven overarching qualities or indications of the divine calling upon a person's life. Just as gravity is constant upon us, so are these seven holy-weighted, spiritual matters.

COMPULSION

There must be a Holy Spirit compulsion within the person who is called to preach the Word. In other words, there is a consciousness within one's spirit, an awareness of a kind of pressure being brought to bear upon one's spirit. Even though this is hard to describe, there is a disturbance or an unction in the realm of the spirit that your mind is given to the whole question of preaching. Over time, this compulsion becomes the most dominant force in our lives.

There must be a Holy Spirit compulsion within the person who is called to preach the Word.

This holy calling is something that happens to you, and God acting upon you by His Spirit. It is something you become aware of rather than what you do. In other words, the drive to preach becomes a burden upon the heart that must be fulfilled. It is a holy preoccupation within the soul that causes the one called to step out in faith and embrace the work.

This divine calling grips the soul and governs the spirit. It becomes an overwhelming obsession that cannot be discarded. It will not go away nor leave a person to himself. There becomes no way of escape. Such a strong force lays hold of the person that he or she is held captive. Eventually, you will be faced with the reality that you are called to preach the gospel and you have a choice to obey or disobey, surrender, or run.

Every ministerial calling was preordained by God before the person was born. So when you were born, God "hardwired" you with certain characteristics that go with the calling. They are inseparable from you as a person.

Being a pastor, evangelist, teacher, or missionary is not simply to have the title or receiving a degree from a Bible college or seminary. Your personality, way of thinking, the way you conduct yourself, etc., are all hardwired to your calling.

For example, a pastor will be an extrovert, always looking to care for others, and will be a leader. An evangelist cannot help himself from always thinking about winning souls. A teacher likes to study and is very organized. A prophet hates evil and things that go against the will of God. An apostle will be driven to help more and more people grow and mature in the things of God. These are traits that are not studied; they are a part of who you are and cannot be changed any more than you can change the color of your eyes.

COUNSEL

Additionally, there will be outside influences that will come to the one called by God. There will be input and counsel from other believers to the one destined for the ministry. It may be the feedback of a pastor or the affirmation of an elder. It could be the encouragement of another believer. When they hear this person speak the Word, perhaps in a class or Bible study, they are often the best discerners of the man who is called into the ministry.

In other words, Spirit-sensitive people often recognize the hand of God upon the person who has been called to preach. Those who best know God and most love His Word often can detect who is being set apart for this work. They give insightful affirmation to the individual being called.

In order for there to be a true call to the ministry, there must be an irresistible, overwhelming craving and raging thirst to preach the Word.

Read carefully what Pastor Spurgeon said to his students:

*If any student in this room could be content to be a news-
paper editor, or a grocer, or a farmer or a doctor, or a
lawyer, or a senator, or a king, in the name of heaven and
earth let him go his way; he is not the man in whom dwells
the Spirit of God in its fulness, for a man so filled with God
would utterly weary of any pursuit but that for which his
inmost soul pants. If on the other hand, you can say that
for all the wealth of both the Indies you could not and dare
not espouse any other calling so as to be put aside from
preaching the gospel of Jesus Christ, then, depend upon it,
if other things be equally satisfactory, you have the signs
of this apostleship.*

CONCERN

When a person has experienced the divine call of God, they
will possess a loving concern for others. God gives to the one
chosen to preach an overwhelming compassion for people. As
part of this divine choice, the Holy Spirit imparts a consuming
desire for the spiritual welfare of others. The God-given call
always includes a concern about others, an interest in them, and
a realization of their lost estate and condition, and where they
will spend eternity. We are called to point them to the way of
salvation.

This love for others includes the distinct realization that
countless people are perishing without Christ. What is more,
there is a concern that many of these lost souls are in the church.
The one called to preach feels compelled to awaken them to their
need for Christ. He or she is constrained to reach them with the
saving message of the gospel.

God-called ministers have a much deeper desire for the
things of God. We are willing to die to our desires and ourselves.
We are willing to sacrifice more for the sake of others. We are
willing to seek out the will of God when others are having fun.
We are willing to ask God to convict us when we are wrong. We

are willing to ask God to deal with us in the area of holiness. The average Christian is willing to sacrifice things for God. The minister is willing to sacrifice himself for the purposes of God.

COMMUNICATION

Out of all the qualifications of an elder in 1 Timothy 3, it's notable that all the ones listed there are also qualities that are generally expected of all Christians. Certainly, elders are to be more mature in those qualities so that they can be examples to the flock. However, elders are to be "able to teach." Nowhere else do we see this as being expected of all Christians. But elders are to be able to teach God's people.

You will not be truly efficient in ministry if you are not "able to teach."

You will not be truly efficient in ministry if you are not "able to teach." It should be our ambition to be "good stewards of the manifold grace of God." We all know certain able ministers who are expositors of the Word, and instructors to believers. We always take something away when we hear them. We come away from such preaching feeling that we have been to a good school. We need to have an edifying ministry!

At the same time, teaching is not the full extent of the pastor's ministry. Other qualifications and abilities are also required. Spurgeon reminded his students:

Mere ability to edify, and aptness to teach are still not enough. There must be other talents to complete the minister's character. Sound judgment and solid experience must instruct you; gentle manners and loving affections must sway you; firmness and courage must be manifest;

and tenderness and sympathy must not be lacking. We must be strong to lead, prepared to endure, and able to persevere. In grace, you should be head and shoulders above the rest of the people, able to be their father and counselor.

CONSTRAINT

There is an overwhelming constraint within the one called to do this work. He or she feels hemmed in to do this work. It is as though God will not let him be released from his duty to preach. There is nothing else he or she can do but pursue this inner drive to preach. Necessity is laid upon him or her, and he or she must preach regardless of what others may say. We must minister the Word, no matter what obstacles must be overcome.

One of the most satisfying yet demanding professions is Christian ministry. However, unlike other professions, you don't choose Christian ministry; it is God that chooses you. The Bible says that Jesus is the head of the Church (Colossians 1:18), and it is He Himself who chooses who should enter full-time ministry (Ephesians 4:10-11).

No one should enter ministry on a whim or just on a desire to do good, or for financial gain. If you are not called, you will not have the grace or the gifting to do it. As a result, you will be frustrated, the life of God will not be present, and it will be just a job, without satisfaction. Someone with a calling to ministry, working another job, will be miserable. Someone not called to ministry, working in ministry, will be equally miserable.

CONTRITION

The person who is called to preach comes under a sobering humility. This person is overwhelmed with a deep sense of his unworthiness for such a high and holy task and is often hesitant to move forward to preach for fear of his inadequacies.

The person who is called by God is a person who realizes what he or she is called to do, and so realizes the awfulness of the task that he or she often shrinks from it. Though we are compelled to preach, we are similarly fearful of doing so. We are sobered by this weighty assignment to speak on behalf of God. We tremble at this stewardship entrusted to us and the accountability that comes with it.

Unlike other professions, you don't choose Christian ministry; it is God that chooses you.

Here's where ministry is different from any secular calling. In secular callings, you can work hard, learn skills, and accomplish great things in the world. But when it comes to the work of ministry, if your goal is to see sinners saved and see Christians edified and mature in Christ, then you are utterly dependent on God and the work of the Holy Spirit. You walk into that pulpit, week after week, utterly powerless to accomplish that task on your own. That's what you're signing up for!

CONFIRMATION

As Paul writes in 1 Corinthians 3, "I planted the seed, Apollos watered it, but God made it grow. So neither he who plants nor he who waters is anything, but only God, who makes things grow." In other words, in all of our ministry, we are utterly dependent on God for any spiritual life, any spiritual growth. And we should hope to see God work through us before we are confirmed in our call to ministry.

There must be some measure of conversion-work in preaching ministry before you can believe that preaching is to be your lifework. It is a marvel to us how people continue at ease in preaching year after year without conversions. Is it their belief that Paul plants and Apollos waters, and that God gives no increase? We believe vain are their talents, their philosophy, their rhetoric, without the signs following. How are they sent of God who bring no men to God?

That's not to say that we should ever presume on God's work or try to manipulate people to respond to the gospel. At the same time, no preacher should be content with a ministry that never sees anybody converted or edified.

Pastor Spurgeon articulates:

I hope it will never get to be your notion that only a certain class of preachers can be soul-winners. Every preacher should labor to be the means of saving his hearers. The truest reward of our life work is to bring dead souls to life. I long to see souls brought to Jesus every time I preach. I should break my heart if I did not see it to be so. Men are passing into eternity so rapidly that we must have them saved at once... If our preaching never saves a soul, and is not likely to do so, should we not better glorify God as farmers, or as tradesmen?

When a person is called to ministry, there are supernatural gifts that will manifest in the life of the person. These gifts flow naturally and effortlessly. In fact, they may be so natural to you that you may not be aware you are flowing in this grace, but others will notice.

People will notice your prayers are more effective. When you preach the gospel to others, you are effective. When you speak, people want to hear. You have a deeper understanding of the Scriptures. There is greater authority in your words. There is greater spiritual power and manifestations.

Ultimately, there must be a corporate confirmation to the one called to preach. The man who is chosen by God to preach must be observed and tested by others in the church. Only then may he or she be sent from the church. We learn in Romans 10:13-15 that preachers are "sent," or commissioned by a sending church. The leaders of the church must examine the qualifications of the one set apart to preach and affirm the validity of this call. Hands must be laid upon him in recognition of what God is doing in his life.

Appendix 2

LIVING AND LEADING WORTHY OF YOUR CALLING

Outside the apostle Paul, many key Christian leaders believe Charles Spurgeon, pastor of Metropolitan Tabernacle in London, England, was the greatest preacher who ever lived. On one occasion, Spurgeon told a very moving story of an extremely poor woman who had been a member of his congregation and lived in slum-type housing.

Pastor Spurgeon went to visit her to give her some comfort and help. While he was there, he looked up and saw a framed legal document on the wall and walked over and read it carefully. It was a document transferring amazing wealth to this woman. She didn't even know what it was and had framed it and put it on her wall!

What had happened was that she had taken care of an elderly man; and when he died, he left her his estate. Unfortunately, she was an uneducated woman and did not know what it was. When the bank finally learned about this, they said, "We wondered who the old gentlemen had left his estate to."

When I think of this story, I think of the incredible inheritance the Lord Jesus Christ left us when He ascended to heaven. We need to learn and to live in this inheritance!

It may be that you have not yet discovered what you have in the Lord Jesus. Could it be that you have framed your spiritual gift as a motto on the wall rather than having carried it to the bank to cash it and use it? Or could it be that you have left your gift under the tree, wrapped and unopened and, therefore, unappreciated?

When God saved you, He saved you by His grace, but He did not save you to sit, soak, and sour. He saved you to serve. *But to each one of us grace was given according to the measure of Christ's gift* (Ephesians 4:7).

God has given you a spiritual gift. *But to each one of us grace was given.* The word "grace" is the Greek word "charis" from which we get the word "charismatic." You have a charismatic gift; however, do not think by charismatic that we mean someone who has a ready smile, a firm handshake, and verbal ability. We say, "Well, that man is charismatic. He'd make a good politician." That is a corruption of the word charismatic. The word charismatic merely means a person who has been gifted by grace. *But to each one of us grace* [charis] *was given according to the measure of Christ's gift* (Ephesians 4:7).

You are a gifted child, but you may be like that poor woman who did not understand what the gift that she had received was and did not know how to use it. Therefore, we want to examine how to discover, develop, and deploy your spiritual gift and minister in the body of Christ.

HOW THE GIFTS ARE DELIVERED

The first truth we need to learn is how the gifts are delivered. *But to each one of us grace was given according to the measure of Christ's gift* (Ephesians 4:7).

God has given you a grace gift; therefore, do not insult Him by saying He cannot use you. In the church, there can be no inferiority or superiority. We are what we are by the gift of God.

Everyone has a charismatic gift—a grace gift. A charismatic gift is a God-given ability for service and ministry. However, it goes beyond natural talent. Spiritual gifts are supernatural—supernatural in source, supernatural in nature, and supernatural in purpose.

God has given you a grace gift; therefore, do not insult Him by saying He cannot use you.

You do not choose your spiritual gifts any more than you choose your natural gifts. You can develop your natural talents, but you did not choose them any more than you chose the color of your eyes or the color of your skin. You received them genetically by your first birth, and your talents are genetically encoded in you by that first birth. However, spiritual gifts are given at your new birth and are supernatural.

The gifts are given by the ascended Lord. *Therefore it says, "When He [Jesus] ascended on high, He led captive a host of captives [the devil], And He gave gifts to men [you]." (Now this expression, "He ascended," what does it mean except that He also had descended into the lower parts of the earth?* (Ephesians 4:8-9).

The Lord Jesus descended—He came to this earth, lived a perfect life, suffered, bled, died on the cross, was buried, and rose again. When Jesus Christ died on the cross for us and with His blood purchased our salvation, at the same time He broke Satan's back. Satan's kingdom came crashing down, and he and his malevolent forces were demolished at Calvary.

Therefore, by His death, burial, resurrection, and ascension, the Lord Jesus Christ led captivity captive. Satan had taken the world captive, but Jesus took Satan captive.

The apostle Paul was talking about a Roman triumph. When a Roman general would win a battle for Rome, he would come back into the city for a parade called "The Triumph." The air would be filled with incense and perfume, and he would be riding on his white horse. The priests would be swinging incense and perfume and the people would be giving their praises to the general.

Behind the general would be the conquered kings and generals who would have been stripped naked and chained to the conquering general's chariot wheels. They would be dragged along behind the chariot while the people jeered and mocked those who had been stripped, shamed, and subdued. Their power was gone and their pride lay in the dust. Behind them would be servants bearing all of the spoils of the battle, the riches that had been conquered and brought back to Rome.

The Lord Jesus ascended on high and led captivity captive. Satan's kingdom was ruined and we have been given gifts to battle—our grace gifts to serve our great King—given to us. Never despise or overlook your grace gifts. They are spiritual gifts from our conqueror, the Lord Jesus Christ, who paid an unimaginable price for us.

HOW THE GIFTS ARE DESCRIBED

Now there are varieties of gifts, but the same Spirit (1 Corinthians 12:4). It is the Holy Spirit who gives different gifts to the church. *And there are varieties of ministries, and the same Lord* (1 Corinthians 12:5). Everything is not always done the same way, but it is the Lord who is doing it. *There are varieties of effects, but the same God who works all things in all persons. But to each one is given the manifestation of the Spirit for the common good* (1 Corinthians 4:6-7).

God gave you a spiritual gift, not for your own enjoyment but for your employment. Your spiritual gift is to bless the church, not to bless you. It is a tool, not a toy.

For to one is given the word of **wisdom** (1 Corinthians 12:8). The word of wisdom is supernatural insight into the mind of God. It is not talking about common sense but about uncommon sense. People who have the gift of the word of wisdom make wonderful counselors.

And to another the word of **knowledge** (1 Corinthians 12:8). Knowledge differs from wisdom in that it is the supernatural ability to know and apply the things of God. Knowledge puts wisdom to practical use. Some will have the gift of wisdom and some the gift of knowledge. Those who have both gifts make wonderful leaders and counselors.

To another **faith** *by the same Spirit* (1 Corinthians 12:9). All believers have faith or they could not be called believers for no one can be saved without faith; however, some people have the supernatural gift of faith—mountain-moving faith. These kinds of people are the visionaries and the pioneers, those who are able to think big and believe God for great things.

And to another gifts of **healing** *by the one Spirit* (1 Corinthians 12:9). Note that it states gifts of healings— plural. There are healings for the body, soul, and mind— physical healing, spiritual healing, and psychological healing.

And to another the effecting of **miracles** (1 Corinthians 12:10). We cannot deny that God is a God of might and miracle.

And to another **prophecy** (1 Corinthians 12:10). This is the ability to foretell and forth tell—primarily not to foretell the future but to tell forth the will of God in a particular matter. We do not have to guess about what the gift of prophecy is because we are told the *one who prophesies speaks to men for edification and exhortation and consolation* (1 Corinthians 14:3). Edification means to build people up as in building a building—an edifice— while exhortation means to encourage, exhort, cheer, and fire people up. Consolation means to comfort or hold people up. A prophet is someone who builds up, fires up, and shores up the people of God. Every church ought to pray for God to give prophets to the church—those who can speak for God.

*And to another the **distinguishing of spirits*** (1 Corinthians 12:10). There are a lot of wild and wicked spirits in the world today.

*To another **various kinds of tongues*** (1 Corinthians 12:10). This means the ability to praise God in a language never learned. When someone speaks in tongues in a worship service, the Lord also desires that the message be interpreted in order for the people to be able to understand it so He gave the gift of *the **interpretation of tongues**.*

Since we have gifts that differ according to the grace given to us, each of us is to exercise them accordingly: if prophecy according to the proportion of his faith (Romans 12:6). Ministry is an act of service.

*God has appointed in the church . . . **teachers*** (1 Corinthians 12:28). If you have the gift of teaching, then you should be teaching a class or a group.

*Since we have gifts that differ according to the grace given to us, each of us is to exercise them accordingly . . . he who exhorts, in his **exhortation*** (Romans 12:6,8). Gifted musicians who have not only vocal ability but also the ability to move the heart often have the gift of exhortation as well as those who do visitation.

Since we have gifts that differ according to the grace given to us, each of us is to exercise them accordingly . . . he who gives, with liberality (Romans 12:6,8). This is the gift of **giving**, which is the supernatural ability to make and give money sacrificially and wisely.

Since we have gifts that differ according to the grace given to us, each of us is to exercise them accordingly . . . he who leads, with diligence (Romans 12:6,8). This is the gift of **leading**. We need people who can head up committees and those who can administrate and lead people forward in various ministries.

*Since we have gifts that differ according to the grace given to us, each of us is to exercise them accordingly . . . he who shows **mercy**, with cheerfulness* (Romans 12:6,8). These are people who do hospital visitation and serve in benevolence ministries.

We all have a role in the goal and a part in God's heart!

HOW THE GIFTS ARE DEVELOPED

And He gave some as apostles, and some as prophets, and some as evangelists, and some as pastors and teachers, for the equipping of the saints for the work of service, to the building up of the body of Christ (Ephesians 4:11-12). Not only does God give spiritual gifts to everyone, but He also gives spiritual leaders to the church.

The fivefold ministry gifts are not only representative of distinct people and ministerial offices in the church, but they also reveal five principles for effective ministry today.

The fivefold ministry gifts are not only representative of distinct people and ministerial offices in the church, but they also reveal five principles for effective ministry today. The apostle, prophet, evangelist, pastor, and teacher represent the principles of governing, guiding, gathering, guarding, and garnering, respectively. All of these principles are needed for equipping Christians for effective evangelism.

In the early church, there was not much difference between an apostle and an evangelist since all apostles were also evangelists. However, not all evangelists were apostles since a direct call by the Lord was necessary. John Calvin believed there were times when God would raise up evangelists as substitutes for apostles. In a real sense, "the apostles did not know when to stop being evangelists." Without the ministry of the true New Testament evangelist, the church would die out.

In Ephesians 4:11, the evangelist seems to "denote an order of workers midway between apostles and prophets on the one hand

and pastors and teachers on the other." There has been much scholarly debate as to whether the ministry gifts consist of four or five separate entities. This debate is the result of the definite article being present before all the various leadership gifts except "teachers" (*toùs dè poiménas kai didaskálous*). The one definite article for both pastors and teachers indicates the "close association of functions between two types of ministers who operate within the local congregation." Even though there is an obvious association between pastor and teacher, there are also distinctives in ministry (Acts 13:1; Romans 12:7; 1 Corinthians 12:28). This interpretation is paralleled in contemporary ministry.

Sometimes these ministerial gifts (Ephesians 4:11) did overlap in the early church. For example, Paul functioned not only as an apostle but also as a prophet, evangelist, pastor, and teacher. Christ used Paul in a fivefold gifting of itinerant evangelistic ministry. For Paul, "the work of the ministry is of much greater importance than any hierarchy of officials."

The aim of all ministry gifts in Ephesians 4:11 is for the equipping of God's people for the *work of service, to the building up of the body of Christ* (Ephesians 4:12). The Greek term for equipping (*katartismòn*) means to put right or to put in order. In surgery, it is applied to the setting of a broken bone. Equipping denotes "the bringing of the saints to a condition of fitness for the discharge of their functions in the body, without implying restoration from a disordered state. The evangelist, along with the other four ministry gifts, is to set the local church in order, making each member fit for the work of ministry. In the case of the evangelist, this 'work of service' or 'ministry' is equipping for evangelism." For the local church to be active in evangelism, the body of Christ must be spiritually healthy.

The Greek term for "building up" (*oikodomēn*) refers "to the act of building . . . to build on something, to build further." There is a fourfold equipping or maturing function for the evangelist in the church. Even though not specially stated, these functions are easily applied to the pastor's leadership roles in the local church. For evangelists and pastors to function biblically, their message, motives, methods, and ministry must align with the Christ-given purposes outlined in Ephesians 4:13-16.

If you want God to use you, you must stop just praying for God to use you and become usable. God will then wear you out. Following are five principles to knowing your spiritual gift:

1. **Desire.** What do you enjoy doing? What do you do naturally? What do you feel you do well?
2. **Discovery.** You will discover your gift as you endeavor to do it. Other people will say, "You have the ability to lead in this area." Dr. Harry Ironside, who pastored Moody Church in Chicago from 1929 to 1948, used to say, "It's a sad thing to hear a man who thinks he has the gift of preaching when no one else has the gift of listening."
3. **Development.** You need to stir up the gift of God. Paul told Timothy to *be diligent to present yourself approved to God as a workman who does not need to be ashamed, accurately handling the word of truth* (Timothy 2:15). Your spiritual gift must be developed.
4. **Dependence.** Your spiritual gift must operate in the power of the Holy Spirit. Since your spiritual gifts are supernatural, they operate with supernatural power.
5. **Deployment.** You must put your spiritual gift to work by working with other saints. Your gift is significant as it relates to other gifted people.

HOW THE GIFTS ARE DISPLAYED

What happens when you find your ministry? *We all attain to the unity of the faith, and of the knowledge of the Son of God, to a mature man, to the measure of the stature which belongs to the fullness of Christ* (Ephesians 4:13). When these gifts work together, the body matures and becomes like its head, the Lord Jesus Christ.

This fivefold leadership team is to help the church become mature in **stature**. Their ministry is to be active *until we all attain to the unity of the faith, and of the knowledge of the Son of God, to a mature man, to the measure of the stature which belongs to the fullness of Christ* (Ephesians 4:13). This verse paints a picture of the church maturing into a perfect, full-grown man (*eis ándra téleion*). "This perfection or completeness is proportionate to the fullness of Christ himself." The whole body of Christ is viewed as one new man with one faith in the Son of God. *The faith* is the full message of the gospel. *The measure of the stature* (*métron hēlikías*) indicates a level of spiritual perfection found in the fullness of Christ. The body of Christ is seen as progressing toward its goal of perfection in the fullness of Christ. In short, as Christ inhabits our humanity, we are to display His deity.

This leadership team can help the local church mature in **stability**. *We are no longer to be children, tossed here and there by waves and carried about by every wind of doctrine, by the trickery of men, by craftiness in deceitful scheming* (Ephesians 4:14). In Ephesians 4:13-14, there is a purposeful contrast made between *a mature man* and "children." Instead of spiritual maturity, the picture is of "spiritual infantilism." The immature Christian is "swung around" by the wind and waves of "fashionable heterodoxy." Instability is one definite sign of immaturity.

The apostle Paul knew a lot about being tossed back and forth on the sea, yet it is far worse for Christians to be "whirled around by every gust of doctrine." The concept that Paul teaches is not "physical infants in a boat who are helpless to manage it in waves and wind; but of physical men, who know nothing about managing boats, who are infants amid wind and waves."

This leadership team can help the local church mature in **speech**. *Speaking the truth in love, we are to grow up in all aspects into Him who is the head, even Christ* (Ephesians 4:15). *Speaking the truth* (*alētheúontes*) means "truthing" or "doing the truth" (Wood, 11:59). A mature church does not tolerate error. Mature Christians recognize religious tricksters by comparing them to the truth. They correct the error of these religious charlatans by speaking the truth in love. "Truthing in love" keeps *every joint* (Ephesians 4:16) limber and flexible in the midst of a changing culture. It has been said, "Whatever is in the well of the heart comes out in the bucket of speech." When the heart of the body of Christ is filled with truth and love, Christians will lovingly speak out against all errors in their society.

Each ministry gift should embrace the other for the dual purpose of equipping the church and evangelizing the lost.

This leadership team can help the local church mature in **service**. *From whom the whole body, being fitted and held together by what every joint supplies, according to the proper working of each individual part, causes the growth of the body for the building up of itself in love* (Ephesians 4:16). The ultimate goal of an active, fivefold ministry is a "coordinated body with each member fulfilling his function." This maturing process depends on the truth that the various ministries in Ephesians 4:11 are interrelated.

The whole body of Christ is being "fitted together" and "held together" by each separate "joint." The Greek term for *supplies* (épichorēgías) is derived from *choregos*. He "was the man who met the cost of staging a Greek play with its chorus." It is only when every aspect of the fivefold ministries is working together that the body of Christ receives the full support it needs to do the "work of service." The lifeblood of the body of Christ is love. Each member is to have a loving heart toward the other members of the body of Christ.

The fivefold ministries of the church are to function like an ensemble singing its various parts. They should produce a harmonic sound throughout the church. Moreover, each ministry joint should be limber, not stiff or limited by spiritual arthritis. Each ministry gift should embrace the other for the dual purpose of equipping the church and evangelizing the lost. When the evangelist is biblically, spiritually, and creatively functioning in the contemporary church, the whole body of Christ is more mature in stature, stability, speech, and service.

When I studied human anatomy and physiology in college, I found that we have synovial fluid that lubricates these joints. When the cartilage gets dry and the synovial fluid is not there and the joint gets inflamed, swollen, stiff, and painful, then the body is not lubricated.

What is the synovial fluid? Love. When we love one another, we do not inflame one another, we do get stiff, we do not become rigid. We all have our gifts of God. We become mature in stature—we become like Christ. We become mature in stability—we are not blown about. We become mature in speech—we know how to speak the truth in love. We become mature in service—we serve one another. The body works together!

Appendix 2 taken from, *Living Life From A Heavenly Edge*. Davis, James O. Billion Soul Publishers, 2022.

ABOUT THE AUTHORS

Dr. Timothy Hill has served in national and international Christian leadership for decades. As General Overseer of the Church of God (Cleveland, TN), he serves as Presiding Bishop for over eight million members of the church in 191 countries around the world.

His past service as General Director of World Missions for the Church of God (Cleveland, TN) took him to more than 100 nations of the world giving oversight to a large multifaceted and diverse global ministry. Previous ministry roles include Assistant General overseer and Secretary General of the Church of God; Chairman of the Church of God International Executive Council; and as Administrative Bishop of the Church of God in Southern Ohio and Oklahoma. Prior to entering administrative work, Dr. Hill served as senior pastor of Riveroak Church of God in Danville, Virginia, where he hosted daily television and radio programs. He is a graduate of Lee University, Cleveland, Tennessee, and received a Doctorate of Ministry from Church of God Theological Seminary, Cleveland, Tennessee.

Dr. Hill has authored many books of sermons and has written 200 gospel songs. He is the author of the number one song, "He's Still in the Fire," which was voted Song of the Year by *The Gospel Voice* magazine. He began recording at age 16 and has 18 recording projects to his credit, including many original songs.

Traveling extensively worldwide, Dr. Hill speaks in major denominational and interdenominational conventions and conferences. He is married to Paula, and they have three daughters, Melinda, Brittany, and Tara. He is grandfather to Timothy Brayden, Hailey Taylor, Lucas Reed Maness, Jaxon River Sharpe, and Jameson Hill Sharpe.

Dr. James O. Davis is the founder of Cutting Edge International and Global Church Network, a growing coalition of more than 2,600 Christian ministries and denominations synergizing their efforts to build a premier community of pastors worldwide to help plant five million new churches for a billion soul harvest and to mobilize the whole body of Christ toward the fulfillment of the Great Commission. With more than 650,000 churches, the Global Church Network has become the largest pastors' network in the world.

Christian leaders recognize Dr. Davis as one of the leading networkers in the Christian world. More than 80,000 pastors and leaders have attended his biennial pastors' conference and leadership summits across the United States and in all major world regions. Dr. Davis is considered to be in the *Top Ten Christian Influencers in the World*.

In October 2017, Dr. Davis spearheaded and hosted *The Wittenberg 2017 Congress* in Berlin, Germany. The Wittenberg 2017 Congress celebrated the 500th anniversary of Martin Luther's nailing his 95 Theses on Castle Church door in Wittenberg, Germany. This historic congress brought together more than 650 influential leaders from more than 80 different denominations and every world region.

Dr. Davis served 12 years leading 1,500 evangelists and training thousands of students for full-time evangelism as the National Evangelists' Representative at the National Office of the Assemblies of God. Ministering more than 45 weeks per year for 40 years, Dr. Davis has now traveled over 10 million miles to minister face-to-face to millions of people in more than 130 nations.

Dr. Davis earned a Doctor of Ministry in Preaching at Trinity Evangelical Divinity School and two master's degrees from the Assemblies of God Theological Seminary.

Sermons For Shepherds
Books By Tim Hill

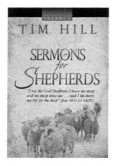

Sermons For Shepherds - Volume 1

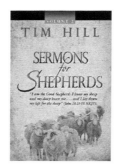

Sermons For Shepherds - Volume 2

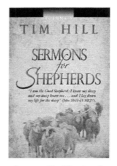

Sermons For Shepherds - Volume 3

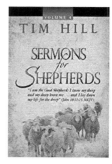

Sermons For Shepherds - Volume 4

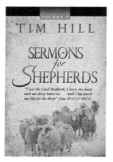

Sermons For Shepherds - Volume 5

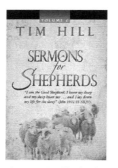

Sermons For Shepherds - Volume 6

Sermons For Shepherds On The Holy Spirit - Volume 7

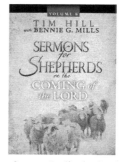

Sermons For Shepherds On The Coming Of The Lord - Volume 8

Available To Order At
timhillministries.com

Books By Tim Hill

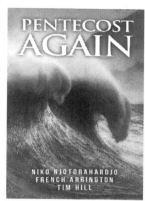

Pentecost Again

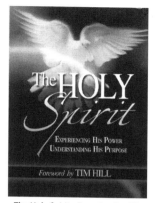

The Holy Spirit - Experiencing His Power, Understanding His Purpose

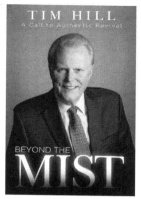

Beyond The Mist - A Call To Authentic Revival

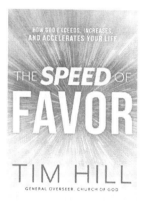

The Speed Of Favor - How God Exceeds, Increases And Accelerates Your Life

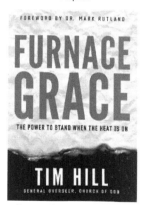

Furnace Grace - The Power To Stand When The Heat Is On

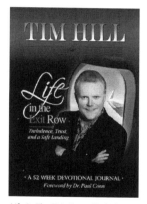

Life In The Exit Row - Turbulence, Trust, And A Safe Landing

Available To Order At
timhillministries.com

MILLION MINISTERS MANDATE®

Carrying The Gospel To The HARDEST PLACES IN THE WORLD

MILLION MINISTERS MANDATE®

CREATING A GLOBAL ONRAMP TO THE HIGHWAY OF MINISTRY TO COMPLETE THE GREAT COMMISSION.

CHECK OUT
MillionMinistersMandate.com

GLOBAL
CHURCH
NETWORK®

ONLINE · ON-AIR · ON-GROUND · ON-TIME

The Global Church Network is the premier community pastors and Christian leaders from 2,700 denominations and 700,000 plus local churches. GCN brings the finest teaching though the Global Church Divinity School (GCDS.tv) and faith-filled training through its Global Hubs of Christianity. GCN synergizes Christian leaders and mobilizes the Body of Christ to finalize the Great Commission!

GCNW.tv

DOWNLOAD THE
GLOBAL **CHURCH** NETWORK
APP TODAY!

Register for events, access resources,
manage giving options, and connect with our team.

GLOBAL CHURCH
DIVINITY SCHOOL

PART OF THE GLOBAL CHURCH NETWOR

IN THE FUTURE, WHO YOU STUDIED WITH
MORE IMPORTANT THAN WHERE YOU STUDI

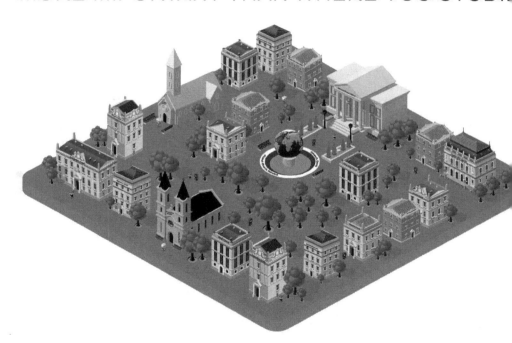

THE BEST **GLOBAL CHURC**
CLASSROOM IN THE WORLD

190 World Class Faculty

GCDS.TV